T0067861

Fool's Gold

Fool's Gold

Selected Modjaji Short Stories

Edited by Arja Salafranca

Copyright for this edition Modjaji Books 2019
www.modjajibooks.co.za

ISBN 978-1-928215-84-4 (Print)
ISBN 978-1-928215-85-1 (ePub)

Cover artwork and Lettering by Jesse Breytenbach
Book and cover design by Monique Cleghorn

Acknowledgements:
NB Publishers for permission to use Jolyn Phillips' story
'The Fisherman' from *Tjieng Tjang Tjerries and other stories*

Contents

Foreword **7**

Botswana Rain WAME MOLEFHE **13**

The Red Earth MEG VANDERMERWE **23**

The Thin Line ARJA SALAFRANCA **35**

Stains Like a Map JAYNE BAULING **45**

In the Spirit of McPhineas Lata LAURI KUBUITSILE **59**

Fool's Gold TINASHE CHIDYAUSIKU **71**

The Outsider ISABELLA MORRIS **79**

Heaven (or Something Like it) SARAH LOTZ **91**

Spying COLLEEN HIGGS **107**

Vicious Cycle RENEILWE MALATJI **113**

Prayers MAKHOSAZANA XABA **129**

The Chameleon House MELISSA DE VILLIERS **145**

Southbound SANDRA HILL **161**

Letter to Management JULIA MARTIN **181**

The Dream of Cats is all about Mice ALEX SMITH **185**

The Fisherman JOLYN PHILLIPS **197**

The Good Housekeeping Magazine Quiz JO-ANN BEKKER **203**

Authors **211**

FOREWORD

A short story is a love affair, a novel is a marriage.
A short story is a photograph; a novel is a film.
— LORRIE MOORE

Short stories are tiny windows into other worlds and other
minds and other dreams. They are journeys you can make to
the far side of the universe and still be back in time for dinner.
— NEIL GAIMAN

There's no other description of the short story that describes it as
succinctly and perfectly as that of the American short story writer,
Lorrie Moore. A snapshot of lives, and without the lengthy commitment of a novel, some say a short story is ideal for our busy, digital-led
lives. They are coming into their own, having faded in popularity
at times, this year alone has seen a plethora of individual story collections being published, which is good news for the form.

Modjaji Books in South Africa, of course, has believed in and
published short story collections almost from the beginning of its
inception in 2007. To date ten collections have been published and
two anthologies, *The Bed Book of Short Stories* in 2010 and *Stray* in
2015. This collected volume of short stories celebrates both the form
and over a decade of publishing short fiction. There's one story each

from the ten individual collections and a handful from the two anthologies, showcasing an enormous variety of stories, styles, voices and talents.

I was both excited and honoured to be chosen to edit this selection of Modjaji fiction. I love the short story – have loved it from my teens and into university, where as part of my undergraduate degree I read short stories for both English Literature and my major of African Literature. While I have always loved the sweep of reading novels, the short story offers something entirely. Within a few pages a writer can evoke a world, a moment or a bright epiphany, that lingers and reverberates long after the initial reading. A writer doesn't need a novel to tell a story, or create a powerful impact in their story telling. Who can forget the power and the twist contained in Can Themba's famous short story, 'The Suit' for example?

And the short story is remarkably flexible – ranging from microfictions of a page or two – to more conventional lengths to the sinuous, winding length of an Alice Munro story, which contain novel-like worlds in them. There are stories that verge on novella-length works, and there are novellas that might just as easily fit into either classification. But whatever the length, they are, as Gaiman notes, 'tiny windows into other worlds' that still allow you to be back in time for dinner. They provide instant hits, so to speak, without the commitment of following a novel's plotlines – perfect for commutes, whether reading on a bus or train or listening to an audio book in a car, and perfect for our time-poor lives. Or, read a short story before bed.

There are stories that are so full of meaning and depth that they been filmed as feature-length films or plays. The list here is long. Again I'm thinking of 'The Suit', which has had been performed many times. And there's the equally powerful 'Brokeback Mountain' by E Annie Proulx, which was made into a successful movie. And there are others, so many others.

Ranging from deep immersion into other lives, highlighting relationships, peoples' motives, societal problems, Aids, poverty, orphaned children, dementia, resilience, to stories of humour and pathos, the following fictions are delightfully varied.

In Meg Vandermerwe's 'The red earth' we are witness to the thoughts and fears of a woman with living with Aids, her sense of isolation and fear palpable throughout. Meanwhile in Reneilwe Malatji's 'Vicious Cycle' the woman narrator ponders the problem of so many absent fathers in a story that sensitively explores this issue.

Relationships form the backbone of many of the stories. In my own story, 'The Thin Line' I explored the fissures and cracks that seep into relationships – friendship or romantic – and break open bonds that we thought might last forever.

Similarly, Wame Molefhe's 'Botswana Rain' is a mediation on the compromises inherent in some lives and some relationships, where it is necessary to be thought 'normal'.

Colleen Higgs takes us back to the Yeoville of the early 1990s with 'Spying' in which a twentysomething narrator remembers the love she took so long to get over, with bitter-sweet memories. This story perfectly captures the hopes and dashed innocence of the narrator.

And in Jo-Ann Bekker's 'The Good Housekeeping Magazine Quiz' the story is told through a magazine quiz format in which a woman can see only too clearly the threat her husband's former lover poses to her marriage.

A deeply poignant story, Makhosazana Xaba's 'Prayers' examines childhood through the prism of a thirteen-year-old looking after her four-year-old sister, both parents having passed away within months of each other. The same youthful resilience is displayed in the young girl at the centre of 'The Fisherman' by Jolyn Phillips, who needs a job fishing, as her father did, casting her line into the waters of luck.

A group of young South African women share a flat and cadge for whatever the cash they can to live on in 'The Chameleon House' by Melissa de Villiers, in a story that has a deeper, darker heart at its core.

And then we're pulled into the past, into 1923, in 'Southbound' by Sandra Hill, in a wry story about an Englishwoman's life in Durban, as told through the various viewpoints of others, and their theories about her life.

Moving on from these debut volumes, *The Bed Book of Short Stories* is centred on the theme of 'bed' and bursting with a variety of stories tha imaginatively interpret this theme. It contains a wide range of writers' voices – both well-known and just starting out.

There's Lauri Kubuitsile's wonderfully humorous 'In the Spirit of McPhineas Lata', which centres on the sexual prowess of the late McPhineas, well-known bachelor, and the village men's desire to emulate his success with their wives.

Equally humorous is 'Heaven (or Something Like It)' by Sarah Lotz in which a woman returns from the spirit world to her old flat, and settles right back in, watching TV 24/7 and puzzling the tenants who take on the place.

There's 'Stains Like a Map' by Jayne Bauling, which focuses on a bed purchased by a young Mozambiquan couple, a bed which follows them through marriage and into a clandestine new life in South Africa with all its challenges – the bed here is metaphor for life itself.

Isabella Morris's 'The Outsider' is a haunting and achingly poignant story of a young woman looking for something less than love with the army guys who pass through the Free State town she lives in.

'Fool's Gold' by Tinashe Chidyausiku is another story that catches you in the solar plexus – the story arcing over a day in the life of a young man eking out an existence carrying baggage for others.

The latest short fiction anthology from Modjaji, *Stray*, themed around the subject of animals. This volume showcases two of the stories from that book. Julia Martin's 'Letter to the Management' tells the story of a mother's dementia and her daughter's awareness and guilt that although her mother's memory is gone, she is still aware of her less than ideal surroundings. Alex Smith's 'The Dream of Cats' is the moving story of a lonely man's meaningful encounter with a street cat, and the effect animals can have on our lives.

Reading and re-reading these stories was a powerful immersion into the variety of fictional worlds offered in these debut collections and the anthologies. The story is both photograph and love affair, and these varied pieces hold up a mirror to our lives and the places we live in.

ARJA SALAFRANCA
JOHANNESBURG, OCTOBER 2019

Botswana Rain

WAME MOLEFHE

It was my mother who rang to tell me. She called at that ungodly hour of the night when messages of birth and death were usually conveyed. I felt the vibration of my cell phone on the bedside table.

"Sethu," she said when I said hello, "I have sad, sad news for you."

I knew then that it was serious. It was rare for my mother to call me by the name she used when I was a little girl, rarer for her not to know the right words to say.

"Kgomotso is gone."

"What do you mean Mama?"

"She passed away."

"No Mama... How...When?" I whispered, pressed the cell phone to my ear, and waited for her to speak. I listened to her breathing, heard my heart beating in my head. I regretted asking the cause of Kgomotso's death, but I needed to know, even though I myself despised the way Botswana people probed the cause of a person's death the way a nurse felt your arm, searching for the right vein from which to draw blood.

"She committed suicide. They found her body yesterday. The funeral will be on Saturday. And, Sethu, she left you a note."

A note? Why did Kgomotso take her life and why did she leave me a note? Fear frothed in my stomach like cola when you drop a pebble in it.

My husband, Thato, lay fast asleep beside me. He slept like our baby did, mouth slightly open, an arm cradling his head.

What if Kgomotso's note exposed my secret? I stole out of bed, taking care not to wake him, wondering if I would ever sleep so soundly again.

When I was a little girl, life was well-ordered. Winters were cold and dry, summers were hot and moist – the way my Geography textbook said Botswana weather should be. When it rained, I raced outside and squelched the mud between my toes. I waved my fingers in the air shouting "Rain, rain make me grow," as I chased after corn crickets that appeared with the rainbow, like marching soldiers.

After the rain, I played football barefoot in the sand, and didn't care that people mistook me for a boy. When the sun got too hot, I rested in the shade with my legs drawn up, my elbows on my knees. Mama would creep up behind me and clap her hands, like crackling lightning, saying, "Sethunya! Sit properly. You are not a herd boy." I'd straighten my legs, and press my thighs together, trying to be more of a lady.

Back then, Kgomotso was my best friend. I was ten when her family moved into the house on our cul-de-sac. We liked lying on our backs together under the *morula* tree, holding hands, sucking on its yellow fruit. She was a dreamer, even then. I would tell her a silly story and laugh out loud. She'd say: "Shhhh Sethunya. Listen. The wind is whispering my future to me… listen. It says one day I'm going to fly to a faraway land where I'll be whatever I dream."

When my boy-hips filled out, my buttocks grew rounder and softer and the *morula*-sized knobs in my chest swelled, Mama said, "Boys are trouble. Run from trouble."

But she needn't have worried. Boys? They did not interest me. I was happiest when I was with Kgomotso and I did not want to share her. When all the girls in my class were whispering and giggling about boys, wondering who was going to ask who to the school-leaver's ball, I really didn't care. But all the same, I played the game. I did not want to be the odd one out.

As I grew older, life tested me. Home. School. Church. Everywhere, it seemed as if I was being cast into a mould. In school I had to memorise what made dust different from dirt. I struggled to remember whether to sweep first then polish, or polish first then sweep. At home, Mama asked: "What kind of a woman are you going to become?" As I grew older, she graduated to: "Oh my Lord, what kind of a wife will she make?" I tried hard to be an obedient daughter, a good woman.

Every Sunday, I dressed up in my floral two-piece to attend the early morning church service. Whenever Father Simon warned "Hell is hotter than fire" and "Cast out the devil," I felt flames singeing my body. I twisted and turned in my seat. I taught Sunday school, sang in the church choir and I feared the Lord. I so wanted to be God's child and I had to go to heaven where everyone was family and everyone was happy.

I tried hard to douse that thing in me that caused me to lie awake at night, longing to be with Kgomotso, but I could not say no to her. When she held me close and pressed me to her, I promised that it would never happen again.

My love for Kgomotso was like Botswana rain. Unpredictable. I gave it sparingly. When she responded, I held my love back. Then she would cling to me, like a clump of grass growing deep in the crack of a rock, trying to suck what moisture it could.

But now Kgomotso was dead... No! She had gone to that faraway land that I dreamed of in delicate pinks and pastel greens – where the sun didn't shine so bright and so long that it dried people's hearts and made them hard as biltong. Yes, this thought consoled me.

I relived the last time I visited her. She'd called me, saying she needed to talk. We met at her house. When she hugged me, I let my arms hang limply by my side. She had seemed distant and her words stayed with me after I left, like puddles after the rain, murky and brown, concealing rocks beneath the surface.

"Do you ever think of me?" she wanted to know.

"Sometimes."

"Do you love him?"

"But of course. He is my husband."

"Maybe you could still come and visit... sometimes?"

I did not respond.

"Do you ever think of killing yourself?"

Her question had shocked me, but I said, "Never. Suicide is a mortal sin," using my Sunday-school-teacher voice and my words stemmed her questions. She made me coffee, put in two sugars, no milk – the way I always made it. She watched me as I ate the cake she offered me – chocolate cake, my favourite. But soon the silence between us became unbearable.

I left.

Although I did not want him to, Thato went with me to Kgomotso's funeral. He was my husband and he always did what was right; that was his way. We drove in silence from our home to hers. I stared out of the window, worrying about what Kgomotso's note might reveal.

Her home seemed further away than I remembered, but maybe it was because Thato drove slowly. Rain had gouged out the surface of the road, creating a patchwork of grit, tar and potholes. As we approached her home, I saw a woman sitting alone in the shade of the *morula* tree, where I used to sit with Kgomotso, pretending to the world that we were just friends.

Sitting beside Thato as he drove, I thought back to when I met him. I was twenty-three. He had just returned from overseas. He played the organ and sang in church. I fell in love with his voice. When he sang, the notes rose from deep in his throat and filled the church. He laughed easily. His shoulders were broad and he towered over me, and I had to tilt my head to look into his eyes. He'd been walking me home after choir practice for a few weeks. One evening he asked, "Do you have a boyfriend?"

"No."

"How come? How can a girl so beautiful she was named "flower" not have a boyfriend?"

"Maybe I was waiting for you," I said and smiled.

He laughed, took my hand and turned it over in his. Then he stroked my palm. My hand seemed so tiny in his but his touch was gentle, like a woman's. "I like you," he said, "a lot."

I smiled. Thato liked me. Out of all the women whose dreams he touched, he chose me. I thought of Kgomotso and I snatched my hand out of Thato's. He looked at me and said, "Sometimes I look at you, Sethunya, and wonder whether you are here with me."

"Ao? Re mmogo, Thato. I am with you. You have never seen me with anyone else, have you?"

He shook his head and said, "One day, Sethunya, you will take me with you, to that place where you go."

I smiled. It seemed simpler than finding words for something I couldn't explain. In that moment, I learnt that lying was easier done in my mother tongue.

After a year of dating, Thato sent his uncles to my house. I arrived home to the smell of rum-and-maple tobacco. Thato's pipe-smoking uncle had come to our home to tell my uncles that their nephew was looking for a segametsi, a bearer of water. Even before his pipe's aroma had left the room, Mama called Father Simon and announced "Sethunya is to be married." A month later, ten head of cattle arrived, on the hoof, with Thato racing behind them. Our families had spoken. I would be Thato's wife.

I saw pride in the way Mama swung her hips on her way to the front pew in church. She held her head upright as if she was balancing a bucketful of water on it. I heard the pride when she trilled her notes higher than everyone else when we sang the final verse. I felt her pleasure as she caressed the soft silks she said would make me a lovely bridal gown.

Her excitement was contagious. I wore a white wedding dress with a long zip and darts that lifted my breasts and skimmed my thighs on its way down to my ankles. It had a sweeping train that brushed all my doubts under the red carpet that led into the church. I repeated after Father Simon that I would love and obey my husband, in sickness and in health, and recited all the other words meant to define marriage.

When Father Simon said "I now pronounce you man and wife," Thato eagerly lifted my veil to kiss me. I smiled, a demure smile, befitting of a good woman. With my hand clasped in his, we danced to "Fiela, fiela, fiela ngwanyana" as ululating strangers converged on us while we greeted the congregation, man and wife. It began to drizzle as we emerged from the church. Tiny raindrops mixed with confetti and everyone agreed we were blessed.

"Remember to thank the Lord for giving you such a wonderful husband," my mother said.

On the first morning of our married life, as I lay next to Thato, gentle raindrops tapped on the windows like a timid man's knock. It was a change from the Botswana rain I knew that usually boomed and thundered as if God raged.

I twisted my hand this way and that and watched my ring sparkle. I wanted to lie still in bed and listen to the rain; listen to my thoughts. When I closed my eyes I smelt coconut and strawberry. I remembered Kgomotso and smiled sadly.

"Tell me, Sethunya. You know you can tell me what is on your mind," Thato whispered as he traced my lips with his finger.

"Ah, I'm just happy for the rain," I said, but his words stole the smile from my eyes and I slid out of his arms. I would have stayed in bed if he had not spoken and soiled my memories.

When Thato told me he loved me, I held my body in expectation of another feeling: the feeling that swept me up on a wave when Kgomotso skimmed my neck with her lips. I smelt the sweet coconut in her hair, tasted the strawberries on her lips. My nipples stiffened as if pecked by a cold breeze and I felt warm in places whose names I did not say out loud. Then she took my hand in hers and we lay together on her bed, soaring to the lands I had only dreamed of.

I was thinking of Kgomotso as I lay next to my husband; thinking how silence did not threaten her, did not disquiet her like it did Thato.

I remembered how I had told her about him. It was a Sunday, after church, the day I usually visited. I waited for her to settle into the couch and then I took the chair furthest from her.

"How do I say this? You know that I have been seeing Thato, don't you?"

"Seeing him? You said he was a good friend."

"He is a good friend... a very good friend. He has asked me to marry him. I have said yes. We are going to move. He's got a job, in Johannesburg."

She looked away, bewildered as a bird that had flown into a window pane. And then she looked at me and said: "Poor Thato. You are making the biggest mistake of your life, Sethunya."

"But, Kgomotso, you knew this would happen one day. How could we go on? I live with the fear of being found out. Imagine the shame. The police… jail…"

"Ah, it's your life. Keep lying to yourself."

I could not respond. She did not walk me out of the house to the gate like she usually did. She had closed the front door as I stepped out. I don't know if she watched me stride down the path to the gate. I didn't look back. What did she know about legitimate love?

I stopped going to her house after that day, avoiding the places she frequented. When I saw her in the street, I greeted her politely, like I did old people, "Dumela mma. O teng, mma?" Whenever her name was mentioned, I pretended not to hear; or I echoed the sounds that other people made when they talked about her. They called her terrible names and said she was trying to be a man. She was sick, they said, and all she needed was a man to cure her. What was wrong with her?

But when I was alone, thinking of Kgomotso filled me with yearning. I thought of her doe eyes that made her look sleepy, and imagined stroking her smooth olive skin and kissing her nose that sat small and pointed in her oval face.

The sun shone at first when we arrived at Kgomotso's home. But as the funeral service progressed, rain clouds gathered like cattle being rounded up. Soon, rain pounded the earth and kicked the smell of just-wet soil into the air.

I had chosen my outfit carefully and covered my dread in the uniform of respectability. I wore a tent-like dress, a shawl across my shoulders, a *doek* on my head and dark sunglasses. Walking beside my husband, my high heels made squelching sounds, kisses to water-logged soil. I was a good Motswana woman.

As they lowered Kgomotso's coffin into the flooded grave, it floated, bumping and banging the sides of the hole. Men took shovels to fill it and the thud of mud landing on the wood fell on my soul. Thato took off his jacket and draped it over my shoulders, and then he too picked up a shovel. I watched the muscles in his arms bunch as he covered my love with soil and I felt tears sting my eyes. I blinked and blinked to keep the tears from falling.

Kgomotso's mother gave me the envelope when I went into the house to pay my respects. I felt her watching me as I turned it over in my hand and slipped it into my bag. I took it out again and tore it open, slowly:

S.

Just couldn't take it. I'm going to a better place.

Kgomotso

That was all. After reading the words to myself, I folded it away again.

Her words were as bland as the funeral food we had eaten, but I understood. She had signed her name with her characteristic giant loop to the "g" and double lines underneath. I remembered how we used to practise our signatures.

"Don't press down so hard on the paper," I would say.

"I can't do flowery like you, Sethunya."

I wanted to cry till I gasped for breath. I wanted to wear black and lie prostrate like my custom demanded of a widow, cocooned in grief so everyone knew that I had lost a part of me. Instead, I remained dry-eyed like a man. No one said "Ao shame. Poor soul. It will be okay. Just be strong," to me.

I saw Thato looking at me but I didn't offer to give him the note. He didn't ask to see it.

The morning after her funeral, lying in bed next to Thato, I was aching for Kgomotso. I knew now that I should have run away with her; I hoped that one day I would find her in that oasis where everyone was happy.

This was what I was thinking when Thato touched my shoulder. But I moved away from him and closed my eyes.

Then our son called: "Papa."

I watched Thato get out of bed and lift him from his cot. He brought our child, Lerang, to our bed, lay down and laid Lerang on his chest.

We lay together in silence, my husband, my son and me.

The Red Earth

MEG VANDERMERWE

Do you know about TB, Mrs Sithole? Okay, you know about it. Well, because of her Aids, your daughter now has a serious TB infection. And because she has Aids, her body isn't fighting this TB infection the way we'd want it to. According to our tests, yes, it's unfortunately not yet responded to our course of treatment. That's why your daughter's still so sick, so weak. She needs more, another few months of different treatments. We cannot be certain ...

I look into the face of this young doctor. I envy it, fat and healthy like it is. Her hand holding the wooden clipboard with the sheets of paper on it, it is plump and strong. It could do anything that she asked of it. She is not looking at me as she speaks about me. She is only looking down at her pieces of paper, looking at one, then another, then the one on top, her mouth and nose covered with one of their cloth masks. I do not want to listen any more. I turn to look at my mother, who is standing next to my bed. She is wearing a mask too, but in her bright colours, yellow and green, she is like a piece of our home village, a single shoot of bright summer mealies amongst all these cold iron hospital beds and cement walls. Mama, I want to whisper, Mama, I want to go home.

Behind her mask this doctor's mouth is still moving. It moves it moves. I imagine plump, soft lips – I too used to have such lips, white strong teeth that can chew meat, tongue without any sores, body clean of disease. I look again at the old woman, my mother, who has travelled so far to come and visit me in this place today. I want to go home, Mama, that is what I want.

But I cannot go home. I know I am not allowed. The breath of those like me is, according to this doctor and the nurses of this hospital, a kind of poison and it can spread through the air without even being seen. Anyway, I am too weak to walk. These useless legs of mine are carrying me nowhere for the moment. So tired. And when I breathe ... *yo*. Constant fire, bubbling cooking oil in my chest. Cough too. Yes, sure sure, but also the stomach sickness, diarrhoea and swelling caused by so many months of painful injections, and in the end, as this doctor has just admitted to my Mama, they are still useless. Mama, how long? How long have I already lain here like so, a lame dog? Five months, four, or is it already six? I do not know. Every day is just the same for us who live here. After treatment we feel so bad thatm we forget whether it is day or night or week or weekend. We forget that life used to go forward, that once we did feel strong. What we need is a big clock, high on the wall, just to *know* for certain that time is passing, understand? Just to *know*. Look, she cannot hear me, my Mama. She is listening, listening to what this doctor is telling her. That is right, Mama. Your daughter, she is not going home. She is not.

A nurse is approaching. She always moves so slowly, this one, when the doctors call. It is like watching a lazy storm cloud move across the winter sky. I have watched and heard her, heard her speaking loudly, complaining to the other one, the small one with the large backside. *Yo!* She says, these patients are too demanding, these doctors arrogant with all their orders for us. We are only two, two to serve twenty helpless patients, real grown babies. Yo yo! Two pairs of hands. If they want more from us, they must operate, cut us in half!

This nurse, she is gliding closer now. She has brought her trolley with her to take my temperature. Her anger, it is like a porcupine's sharp coat of thorns, it is a thorn under my skin. Why should I look at her? I ask myself. I still have my pride. This great baboon is no friend of mine. Instead I close my eyes, swallow. Pain, fire, raging all over my body. Especially here, where I breathe and when I breathe. And the doctor? Still talking. Words, so many words, talk and talk, talk. Exhausts me. Her bad news, it exhausts me. If only to die in peace, I think. But no, that is not how it is going to be.

'Open your mouth, Bongumusa, open.' It is the angry nurse. Obediently, but with a great effort, I must open for her. 'Wider, wider.' To make room for the long glass thermometer that in my mind is worse than a sangoma's spear being thrust into a helpless ox. Everything hurts, understand. My tongue. To be touched, even to be held with the greatest tenderness. This morning when my mother washed me with the basin of warm water I thought I would cry each time the sponge brushed my skin. For a moment now, my tongue will throb like it has been struck hard, stabbed deep. But I will not show my mother how much her only daughter suffers. She looks, smiles, thinks such things can make me feel better.

I close my eyes. I taste the spear's hot metal. 'Closed, keep it closed. Now open.' I must open it again. This nurse stands. See how bored she looks, bored for all to see. My Mama cannot look at her. See how one fat arm is folded across her large chest and with the other hand she is holding the thermometer with my temperature on it, holding it out to this doctor as though it alone could kill. The doctor looks at it, nods, scribbles something down on her pad. That is right, yes, I know all of their actions already, know them by heart. Now the nurse must wipe it clean. Ha! Clean from me as though these are the old days and I have just given birth and so everything that I touch is now considered dirty. She does this with a tissue. Watch: the tissue and thermometer she will drop into her bucket of disinfectant on her trolley. She will peel off her plastic gloves and drop them in the bucket too. See, she does it just like I say, and takes her trolley and without another word pushes it away and is gone.

Mama, what are you thinking? I can see that you are frowning. You look confused, what are you thinking Mama? I am not the first one that you have watched, not so? How many now? Four. Before me your son-in-law and two older sons. First Fula, soon after Buyisana, then my Sipho. Each one the same story, was it not so, Mama? As ugly as I have become, this body of mine down to its loose skin and its sharp bones.

I know, Mama, I helped to care for them too, remember? And watched them as you now watch me, life slipping through like delicate sand blown away more and more each day until nothing is left. We could do nothing for them, hey Mama. Not even expensive goat's blood medicines. It is true. They are buried now, I can still see the place very clearly. I visit it often in my mind. I leave this useless body of mine and fly down the steep south-facing hill at the back of the house where their graves are marked by small wooden crosses in the red earth.

When the wind comes up from the valley through the village, does it still blows the crosses down, Mama, and do you still send Nomusa to replace them? You should not, she does not like it. She is superstitious, the other children have said things to her in school. You should send Mbimbi.

I have never told you, Mama, but when the fever has been very bad in this place I have had some messages from my brothers and from my husband. They have visited me three times already in my dreams. They have told me: our mighty ancestor's blood that was spilt, the earth drank it, that is why the soil is red. That red earth now also becomes our graves. Soon the earth will grow redder and redder with all the bodies that are being put into it and soon everyone will be able to smell the blood, like wet metal, like rust, like you can smell it when you have slaughtered a goat or an ox. See that one lying next door? That young woman very sick in that bed with her family all around, mother, aunties, sisters? She is dying, I mean she is almost dead. They rest hands on the lumps on the blankets that used to mean her hand, leg, foot. They do not know, but she knows. You know my sissy, hey, I know you do. Know about the blood in the earth. Know what I am talking about? Yes?

One year ago, since ARVs, before this TB, my own death and my grave felt very far away. A year ago what could I still do? Though still I had the Aids, since the tablets, I believed I could conquer it myself and I would conquer it, not only in my own body, understand, but also in all the places of my village and in the surrounding towns too. I wore a t-shirt given to me to wear by one of the charities that came to speak with patients like myself one day at the Aids clinic: HIV-positive. They convinced me to participate in one of their awareness parades and I did it. I could dance, could clap, could stamp my feet and stir the dust. I could sing, could throw my voice towards the sky and watch it roll from hill to hill like thunder and then fall, entering the ears of anyone willing to listen. I had a good singing voice, you know. At one such event one year ago, I remember, I led the singing group. And always in church, I sang at the end and start of the services. The minister would say, 'Sing, Sissy! Sing! Stand up and let the angels celebrate! For Jesus is coming!' My fine singing is gone now, coughed and vomited out.

Before, in the beginning, before the charity with the singing and the songs, I fought back at the people in my village who called women like myself names because they had heard the disease, the Aids, came from having sex with many men while our husbands were away working in the cities. Some women, the people even attacked them with machetes. To see what they did to them, how they hurt them! Because they wanted them driven from their villages, from their towns. Driven out. They thought that they were cursed because that is what some sangomas had said.

But I was courageous, I am telling you now. I had already buried my brothers and my husband. Do not just sit down quietly to die and do nothing, that is what I told myself. Remember Queen Nandi, warrior mother of the great King Shaka. No one would speak of it, but I spoke of it. No one would come near me, to my house, or let me close, but I went to them. Now, more and more often, I have heard from Mama, through the streets of the big towns we know there are awareness parades like I used to sing in before, and in squares, in community youth centres bare as bread, community HIV/Aids drama. So some things are getting better? Yes? I tell myself Yes even though in my heart I am not so sure. Last spring my own children participated in one such spectacle for those with parents and family sick and dying from HIV/Aids. The government posters in the schools and along the tarred roads, they say education can save my children. Save them from death because of the virus. But what can save them from this? And who can save them? A life without mother or father?

These doctors and nurses, they do not really know what to do with us, I know this. They lock us in here like animals, put on their masks and tell us, 'Here, take, take these medicines, take.' So many. But I am not feeling better. 'You will.' Sicker than before. 'Trust, it will come. Now come, we are not giving you these for our own good, hey? Yo! Very expensive, understand? Now come come come, swallow.

Give me your arm your leg so I can put this needle into you.' And the ARVs. No good for the TB, so they are no good but still I take, two times every day. 'Take them too. Come come come. Do not take so long. Swallow, swallow.'

Since the TB has come, there is only that. It has brought with it new things I know. The ARVs, they had made things once again possible for me for eleven months, but now it is again completely impossible. Just to walk by myself, anywhere. Using the toilet without help. And sitting up. Eating solid foods, bread, meat, all that I enjoyed before. I can no longer take milk, chew, sing, talk. Words. Finding the words to talk about things, and even those things seem to be slipping further and further away from me every morning, my real life growing as thin as my body.

I do not know. Do not ask me any more about hope or no hope, I do not know. Yes, it is true, I do still believe in miracles. My name, does it not mean 'She who can put her trust in God'? She who can trust the ancestors, Jesus Christ? They saved me once, from the Aids, made me feel strong again. I could look after my children, could work for them and hold them, could work for the charity. Still now, still now, so close to the end, so sick, I do pray. First to Jesus Christ, then to the mighty ancestors, finally to my own body. But do they have the power to save me again?

I will tell you a secret, the secret of what I pray to my body each morning. 'Listen, body, I pray, listen to me well. I will look after you if you will look after me. I will be good to you if you are good to me too, if you give me power and help me to fight and kill this new disease as our ancestors once slaughtered their enemies. Please, give me the strength to do it. If you keep me strong and healthy so that I can care for my children and protect them, then I will look after you and care for you and never spoil you.' But I do not know if my body can even hear me any more, that is the truth. All I now know is this pain, this fire inside that cannot be put out, and the feeling that I am only just managing to hang on, too scared for the moment to let go. Not for myself, understand. No, for my three children, that is why I fight, that is why I stay here and hope and try. I need to think of my children, understand. To know that first they will be all right. The girls? I hope and pray that they will they be safe. I know they are sensible. They listen to their grandmother, they go to church, they take care with their school studies. But the boy ... only four, too young. The difficult question is, have I put enough into them, into my two girls, taught them enough over these thirteen years, to help them with their younger brother when I am no longer here?

I do not have the strength at the moment to offer my daughters and my son any more lessons. Only to lie here and to breathe and to breathe and to breathe. Each shallow burning breath is a decision to not give up yet. So I hang on for them, to them, my three children. I'm a day trapped, caught, waiting for the sun to set finally or to rise again. Doctor, hey? What do you say? Which will it be?

And you, Mama? I look at you again and again, Mama. You too will not live forever. This morning when you arrived I saw how you have grown very old and tired with all your grief these past years. A woman your age should have many children to take care of her, but instead you are forced to take care of them, your grandchildren too. And the journey? That journey where you carried me here, your grown daughter, to this town's clinic on your back like a baby, was very hard for you. You had to stop many times. If the bakkie had not come along offering us a lift, I am not sure either of us would have made it. I miss my home, Mama. I miss seeing people's whole faces without masks, the faces of those that I love.

But I am not dead, not dead quite yet. Better, stronger still than the dying girl next door. Uncle's buffalo thorn waits. It waits to call my soul back to our homestead. So there are still some things I can do, not so? I still have some choices left. For example, I can choose to lie here quietly, shivering in my body, and decide whether or not I will love it or I will hate it. Sometimes I cannot help it, you know, I love it still, in spite of everything, in spite of how useless it has become, when I remember what my body could do before, how it once was. This morning when I caught sight of my right hand as my mother was washing my fingers gently with the sponge, like clay pottery that might break, I remembered my old self. These hands, that today I can hardly move beneath the sheet, that sometimes will not even hold a cup, they were once beautiful hands, hands with a mind, always busy cooking, carrying, clapping, caressing, sweeping, sewing. These feet walked, stomped, danced. I cannot move my toes, I cannot. But sometimes in my mind I am still performing all those actions that my body now refuses to do and at such times I also wonder if we need bodies at all. No body and you are like the wind – everywhere, free. Only, the wind is lonely too. That is why sometimes it cannot help itself but it must howl. Not last night or today, all is quiet. But sometimes it howls so loudly outside this hospital, I tell you, or tears at people's houses in my village, ripping at our roofs, shaking the hinges of doors and windows, trying to force its way in through the mud, the brick, the grooves, so that it can be with us, touch us, if only for a short while; so no one can deny how lonely the wind really is.

Death, it is lonely, yes. This hospital, a lonely lonely place even with so many other sick people around, shivering and moaning, stinking of our own sweat mixed with the hospital disinfectant. The plump, healthy white and brown faces of the doctors and nurses seem to be in the wrong place. They are the strangers here, the living amongst us pale sweating ghosts. I and the others male and female, young and old, brothers and sisters, of a single, outcast tribe yet each alone, apart. Each alone and apart in his own suffering, understand. I tell you something more, when we catch another's eye, my fellow patients and I, we look without interest. Why be interested? We know that face, know it too well, it is our own.

Everything dies. That is what you learn if you lie in bed all day with nothing to do but look out through the locked window or watch the sick growing only sicker with each new full moon. Everything comes to its end – daylight, sun, night, rain. The plants grow then wither, the food is cooked then eaten, words are spoken then disappear into memory and are eventually forgotten, you are given hope – you will get better, you will be healed – and then it is taken. And my children? What will become of them? Of their lives? I know that once I am gone there will be arguments about my children. Mama tells me the fighting has already started with my brother's wife. I want my mother to keep them but who will listen once I am no longer alive? Not for love, understand. They do not want them because of love but because of the government money grants for orphans. If I think about this too long, if I let myself think on it, God, I am suddenly so very, very angry, so it gives me a spasm, a pain deep deep inside my chest. The fire roars. I taste blood. Then I want to hit, to strike, to bite, to scream and throw myself from this damn bed and run, fall out of this hospital, die on the road back to my village if I have to, because a child, it needs its mother.

I must push myself up. I cannot just be lying here, silent as a lump of stone, a lame dog, any longer while you speak, doctor, I am going home, I am going. To hell with you, doctor. I try to get up, to push myself up but I can only bare my teeth, moan. Yo. She is looking at me now, oooh, yo, she looks very worried, her eyes. No, don't touch me! Don't! Her mouth, what is it saying behind her mask? Now they are coming, taking their time, moving slowly from the other end of the room beside the door. They are shouting something at Mama. Go to school! Don't go to school! Take your schoolbooks, throw them into the stove! Get out! They are shouting at my children back home in my village, Go!

Yes, that is it, that is right! I am upset. But I do not need to rest. No! The doctor is taking Mama, but where? From this room. I watch her, my mother, an old woman swept away with her bag of beans picked for me from the red soil of my people, soil full of blood from bodies and birth-cords and the birth-cords of my own children and all we have already buried, my children too. I watch them all go and see them all, Mama and my children, my husband and my brothers swallowed by a black hole. Soon soon, a country of orphans, soon soon. The nurses are coming, the cloud who passes without knowing what a heavy shadow she casts, the other little one too. Faces like angry farm dogs, both. Their strong hands will push me down and back into this pillow. Their masked mouths will issue me with stern warnings about my health and the health of these other patients. And I am so ungrateful, they cannot believe it. Oh go to hell, man, don't you know we are dying? What have we to be grateful for? I must tell them, I must let these nurses know.

I feel like an orphan myself, understand. Completely alone, that is how I feel. My own children no longer belong to me. My own mother no longer belongs to me. My own body no longer belongs to me. I am an orphan, understand? Apart from everything, everyone.

The Thin Line

ARJA SALAFRANCA

Two women sat at a table in a restaurant drinking herbal tea. Behind one of the women a man smoked, making the atmosphere cloudy. The other woman stirred lemon wedges and brown sugar into her cup – acid and sweetness mingling soothingly on her tongue.

Egg smells lingered.

They sat and talked about life and work, wanting to be free of the grind of everyday existence and how they wished they could stop working – be free to paint, dance, write, be creative.

It wasn't an option for them.

A group of businessmen came to occupy a table near the window. The men were loud, laughing raucously. The women strained to talk above the noise, voices hurting. The tea was getting cold.

The woman who was not involved asked the other how everything was going with her boyfriend. Fine, wonderful, the other replied. There was nothing wrong there. The woman without a boyfriend paused, she looked her friend in the eye, drank a last sip of tea and said: 'People have market value, and I think you can do a lot better.'

The other woman shot back: 'Why?'

The friend, realising that she should not have said anything, replied, 'Forget it. I'm sorry. I don't know what goes on in your relationship. He's good for you in a lot of ways, understands your need to paint, be alone. Forget what I said. Sorry. It's erased.'

'Okay,' the other woman said.

They looked at each other, searching each other's faces. Something had opened up between them, something had stretched wide, wider than it should have, and then it had closed, too suddenly, too abruptly.

One year, some time ago, a man and a woman took a holiday on Lake Malawi. They rented a chalet on the shores of the lake. She was a stockbroker. He was a photographer. They had broken up a few months before going on this holiday and then had come together again after bumping into each other at a shopping mall.

Now they walked along the shores of the lake. The water lapped gently. It was humid. The woman sweated, her hair scrunched into a ponytail. The man walked ahead of her. She came up behind him, kicking up the sand with her effort. She could hardly breathe in this close air. She gasped slightly as she walked behind him.

They had come out after lunch for a bit of exercise. There was tension between them.

They had not fought. They had simply walked along the shores of the lake, sweaty, impatient and tired. The woman was angry. This holiday was not going to restore their hastily repaired relationship. This was clear now, with ten days still to go before the end of the holiday, only a few behind them. She sat down on the sand and squinted into the white distance. He walked ahead, sauntering, not looking back at her. She watched him, admiring his broad back, his legs tanned by the tropical sun. He did look back eventually, eyes hidden behind sunglasses. She could not see the expression behind the shades. He seemed to pause, look at her, then stared into the distance. She watched him as he paused, as though he were sniffing the air, assessing something.

The woman was distracted by a little boy who was trying to sell her something. She took off her dark glasses.

'Ten dollar!' the boy beamed, thrusting a wooden statue at her. On a base of dark wood, the boy, or somebody else, had carved a slim-hipped fisherman, spear raised in one hand. The woman smiled wanly. 'I don't have any money on me now, and I don't have any dollars.'

'Five dollar!' the boy smiled demandingly.

'I don't have any money. I told you. No money.'

The boy smiled at her, held her eyes. Water lapped at her feet. She was hot and sticky. She tried to take a few deep breaths in this coiled thick air. She wiped sweat off her forehead with the raw back of her hand. The boy carried on looking at her.

The man paused again when the girlfriend had become a speck in the distance. He'd walked a long way away from the chalet. He sat on an upturned fishing boat and watched the fishermen hauling in their loads. The sky was dark and the lake was churning, there was a storm coming up and white foam capped the waves. The fishermen smiled at him. The man's camera dangled around his neck. He felt calm. He went toward the fringes of the lake and watched the surface churning up. He looked forward to the rain.

He felt something for the woman he'd left behind sitting on the shores of the lake, staring after him. But he didn't know what. Not concern, not irritation, he felt too detached to be angry or irritated. Regret, yes, regret, that was it, and perhaps sadness. Sadness for her, that she had come all this way, hoping to restore their relationship and it was all too clear that they could not go back, they could not go forward.

Later, he sat in the bar, fans whirring the hot air around the room, and drank beer and thought about the pictures he wanted to shoot on this trip.

It happens at the oddest times; and when you least expect it. It happens when someone says something that is not meant to wound or estrange, but it still does. It could be a dark candlelit restaurant, and a couple are testing the waters, trying to see if they can still be together. And they are sitting in this restaurant, which probably holds memories for them and they can see the desired reconciliation will not take place. Past hurts bristle around the table and the man says he doesn't know what he wants, and the woman says, 'I never enjoyed sex with you, you know.' The man's eyes cloud over. He doesn't know it, and neither does she, but now it is definitely over. His eyes will cloud over further, and then his heart will snap shut. What she has just said will never be erased. It can only be remembered, filed away, used as ammunition.

Except he will no longer need to keep it as ammunition. His snapped heart will harden, although he will only realise this after a few weeks. And he will stop caring and start to realise that her feet are ugly and there are lines around her mouth, and she slouches.

It finally struck one morning over breakfast, over scrambled eggs, toast burning and juice spilling.

'Can't you help!' she yelled as the smell of burnt toast filled the kitchen.

'Yes,' he said calmly, 'I can help.'

He took the toast out from under the grill, spreading thick globs of butter on the blackened surfaces, transferring the crumbs into the butter dish.

'You're getting crumbs in the butter dish,' she said.

'Yes, darling, I am. I'm helping you to make breakfast, dear.'

The dears and darlings hung in the air, bouncing off the woman's startled expression.

'I can't eat that ...' she started. She looked at the toast, the cold, bunched-up eggs in the pan, the dishes in the sink, the sun glinting off the water outside.

'I'm going out,' he said. 'I'm going to eat breakfast at the hotel.'

'You can't do that ...' the woman protested, watching as the man pocketed his wallet, put on sandals and sunglasses and left.

But words grow up and reverberate, and no matter how hard you try to erase them, they come back. They repeat like indigestion. You hide them behind justifications and excuses; but still they repeat, exerting influence.

The words looked back at this other woman and her boyfriend as they hugged, watching each other in the bathroom mirror. He smiled, eyes jovial, sparkly and unaware. She smiled, lines deepening at the corners of her mouth. She had started to notice things: faults in him that she had been able to ignore before. Other things started to grate on her, irritations she had once accepted as being part of living with another person. She tried not to say anything, but gradually she began to criticise him and snap at him over minor details. He was good-natured, he laughed off her bad moods and understood her need to paint. She tried to remember how much she loved him, and sometimes she'd find her love again. Sometimes, and more often, it receded in the tide of irritation and she'd be forced to pretend, to smile and cook and say nice things, hoping her good feelings would return and she would remember her love and forget the comments of her friend who had sprayed words like poison across a table in a coffee shop.

But as the weeks went on she grew sad and could not remember her love, or forget the words, and she started imagining the ending. She saw omens everywhere: it had been nearly a year that they had been together; the cycle was bound to close. They did things they hadn't done in nearly a year, ate a kind of cake they hadn't had since the beginning. The omens were chilling; she tried to ignore them. And they multiplied.

'Please don't leave me,' she said to him one night, and he smiled and kissed her and said that he loved her; he wasn't about to leave her. And they were genuine, those words of his, but still it felt unreal. The weight of sadness and endings grew oppressive. She tried to imagine coping without him, and could not.

Sometimes you have to accept things: it is probably a good relationship, with a man that is kind to you, and you laugh together; he respects your need for privacy and aloneness, and there is love, of a sort, but are you soul mates?

It was the man in the restaurant so long ago who spoke of soul mates, and how he didn't think you were a soul mate, perhaps that's what ended that particular relationship. He was haunted by the idea of finding 'the one', and he had put that desire into you, even as you scorned the idea, and couldn't quite believe in it. It means that here you are, years later, haunted by the need for passion, the need to find your soul mate, whatever that might lead to, whatever that might mean.

When problems crop up, the woman with the boyfriend remembers what her friend said about market value and that she thought the boyfriend wasn't good enough. The line is so thin between desire and lust, passion and liking, love and hate. Friendship hovers somewhere in between.

The couple came back from their holiday in Malawi. The man became a famous photographer. But they did not remain together. They broke up for the second time soon after returning to Johannesburg. Three months later she met the man she'd marry and have three children with. She did not forget the photographer, nor did she forget her love for him, imagining it moved in her still. At night, with the children asleep in their beds, and her husband beside her, she'd lie awake, waiting for the sleeping pills to take effect. She would think of that other man, the photographer with golden shoulders, tanned legs and a future ahead of him. She'd remember him that day at the lake, the way he had walked away from her, not looking back. It was over then, they both knew it. It was as though he was already imagining another future. But it had not been over for her. She had watched him go that day, not really believing that this was the end. A young boy had tugged at her arm, demanding dollars she didn't have, in the same way that her lover no longer had any feelings for her. She had not cried that night, nor for the rest of that badly planned holiday. Love had turned to indifference and then to a vague, porous hate almost as easily as the attraction had begun.

So, at night, this woman will lie beside her husband and she will listen to his heavy breathing and she will gently touch him, because, yes, she loves him, but it is not the same. It cannot be the same. She will never fall out of love with that photographer, even though her husband loves her, and she, as his wife, loves him. When they fight she imagines the photographer divorced, wanting her again, begging her to see him, start up something new. But as she sighs she knows that will never happen. The thin line between love and hate fades and evaporates.

What is that moment, that final act that causes something to snap, what makes hate follow love? Who knows? A certain expression used too often. A bad temper in the morning, every time you yell because the toaster's dial is set too high and he, or she, keeps forgetting to turn it down to a lower temperature. There's also the shower door left hanging open once too often, and there's the need for solitude and independence, sometimes saying yes when you mean no.

Yet there are other relationships where the toaster is set too high and the shower door is open all the time, but it's okay somehow, because somewhere there's love and somehow that love keeps growing. The love mutates into acceptance, tolerance and muted passion. There's no way of knowing why or how it happens. It's simply there, through mornings of spilled coffee and rushed goodbyes, through deciding what to have for dinner, shopping when the sky's already turned dark because you've both worked so late.

A woman is having coffee with her friend. The one, the woman with the light brown hair, has a boyfriend. The other, with the dark brown hair, does not. She has lost weight. The other has put on weight. She is not happy about it, and her boyfriend tells her not to worry, but she minds and the extra weight is heavy on her. She does not like tight clothes or her breasts bulging out of her bra. She won't buy new clothes until she's lost weight. But it isn't happening. It's nearly a year later. They sit in the same coffee shop, this time they drink cappuccinos; the thinner friend drinks hers with low-fat foam. The other indulges in full-fat foam, there are no more pretences; there is little need for low-fat milk when she's putting sugar in her coffee instead of sweetener and she'll probably have dessert later on.

They talk. The one woman has now moved in with her boyfriend. The other still doesn't have a boyfriend but is moving on in her life in other ways. Outside the sky is brown and grey, threatening rain. They talk about therapy, the influence of parents and how they hurt their children when they're just trying to express love. It is a long discussion, they both open up, pouring out emotions and experiences they have not shared before. There is some discomfort, some embarrassment. They talk around the issues. They have moved on. They talk about the boyfriend, about living together, how all the potential problems of divorce manifest in your twenties when you're first loving and sharing homes with men.

The one with the boyfriend has never lived with a man and is finding the experience strange. There are all sorts of masculine habits that she's never had to live with, she's never quite sure if these are normal or not.

They do not talk about the suitability of the boyfriend, or the possibility of marriage. Whether they skirt the issue out of fear of opening up a rift that shouldn't have been touched at all, or whether they skirt it because there are more interesting things to talk about is unclear. They are older and another year will be dying soon.

The coffee shop is empty now. It's muggy, the afternoon stretches out, there's another month to go before the new year, and the decisions that await them. They sip coffee and talk, looking into each other's eyes, connected by a thin thread of like.

Stains Like a Map

JAYNE BAULING

We bought our bed in Maputo just before we were married. I suppose it was really a mattress, but it was all we would have to sleep on, so we called it our bed. I was glad it was still safely sealed into its plastic bag for the long and dusty bus ride back to our village. I wanted it to be perfect the first time we shared it.

We're not tall people, so our bed was long enough, but we had to lie like one person, holding each other tight and hard unless we wanted to roll off onto the floor. It wouldn't have mattered if we had. Our bed was only a few centimetres high, a strip of yellow foam rubber, but the holding on was fun if we weren't fighting. If we were, Ido would sit outside and I would find our bed suddenly too wide.

That was in the beginning, when the bed was new. The foam was pale yellow, fresh and firm and unmarked, like a page waiting for writing. The first stains were ours, our mouths and fingers added to the damage. You know how it goes. We were practising for making Niando. The yellow began to darken, in the way of foam rubber, I don't know why that happens. Us-shaped dents and hollows appeared. Mostly I liked them. Just occasionally I missed being one instead of two, me instead of we. Often, during the holding on, I would pretend to myself that our bed was a small boat in which we were drifting on a terrible sea, and if one of us fell off we would pull the other down too, among the strangling seaweed or into the jagged mouths of sharks.

Sometimes I felt that was our real situation anyway.

About four months before Niando was born, I started picking fights with Ido to get the bed to myself. I could hardly believe the way my belly was swelling. My size made sharing hot and uncomfortable. I think Ido might have been glad not to share too.

When Niando was born, just before we came to South Africa, he arrived so suddenly that only Ido's mother was there to help me, and so our bed soaked in more stains. When Ido got the message to come home and he saw his son, he couldn't speak for an hour. He smiled a lot though.

When I washed our bed, it looked fresh and new again, but after a few weeks faint outlines started to show, like the ghosts of stains.

The first time we tried to come to South Africa, the truck never arrived at the meeting place. A man who called himself an agent had made us pay in advance, so trudging back to the village with all our belongings and Niando crying all the way, I should have been as angry and upset as Ido. I'm not sure why I wasn't. My feelings about going to South Africa weren't as positive as his, but they weren't exactly bad feelings either.

After that, every arrangement we made fell through. Things kept going wrong. Once we set off and the car we'd paid for broke down. Next there was another truck, but three days before we were supposed to leave the floods started and the roads were washed away. I started believing we weren't meant to leave Mozambique, but Ido and some of the other men from the village were determined to go. After three months of trying, they decided we should walk.

Ido tied up our mattress in a roll that bounced against his back. Sometimes, for a change, he would take Niando and I would have the bed for a while. It wasn't heavy, but I'd get so hot with it bumping behind me, I'd start imagining I was melting and that soon the only thing left would be a small puddle of me.

First we walked north a bit, so that we could cross the big river while we were still in Mozambique, openly using one of the bridges. We were all worried that the man who called himself a guide wouldn't be at the meeting place we'd arranged, and that it would be more money lost, but he was there waiting for us in the smoke-coloured evening. Just for a moment I was disappointed, but I didn't let it show. I felt angry with myself, as if I was being disloyal to Ido.

The guide didn't come all the way with us, just far enough to show us the opening in the fence. Even in the dying light I could see the path beaten through the long grass by others who had come that way. It made me wonder just how many had gone through before us, and if they had found work and shelter. Would there be something left for us?

We were mostly too frightened to sleep once we entered The Park. Only the babies slept, worried to constant waking by mosquitoes. The rest of us would sit close around our fire when we felt it was safe to light one. We would listen to the night, wondering which sounds came from predators, which from prey. There is a sobbing sound you hear in the bush at night that Ido said came from some night bird, but there is laughter too, somehow lonelier than the sobbing; there is a long-drawnout whistling and a shrill screaming, all woven about and between the roaring and barking. Sometimes you think there is silence, but it is full of small sounds, sighs and rustlings and slitherings and squeaks.

In was in the hottest part of our third day walking that I heard a sharp little sound behind me, like a gasp of pain. When I turned I saw that Nelita had stopped. Her pregnancy slowed her down and she and her husband always fell behind.

'The baby!' She stared at me out of frightened eyes. 'It's coming.'

'It's too soon.' Her husband Pekiwa sounded angry, not wanting to believe it.

'Are you sure?' Valente asked.

The men all started shouting that she must be mistaken and that she couldn't have a baby out here. I gave them one of my looks.

'Babies come when they come, not when men say they should. Remember how Niando didn't wait for you to be there?' I said to Ido, already handing Niando over so that I could help Nelita.

She and her husband were travelling with only a sleeping bag, so I unrolled our foam mattress, trying to escape the noon heat in the patchy shade of a clump of thorn trees. We had no water left so Pekiwa went to look for some. We were worried about the smell of blood, and at first Nelita was brave the way she bit back her screams when the contractions got bad, but when Pekiwa didn't come and didn't come, she seemed to stop caring about anything. The baby was a feeble thing, its legs and arms like little sticks, and too weak to take my milk when Nelita turned away from our attempts to put it to her breast.

Did she blame the child for the hours passing empty of Pekiwa's return?

'She won't feed,' I fretted to Ido. I had I tried again after Niando had drunk his fill and was quiet, only stirring to scratch at mosquito bites in his sleep.

'It could be that she senses you aren't her mother,' he suggested.

'It's not that. It's because she came so early. She can't suck.'

'If Pekiwa doesn't come back ...' Ido didn't say any more.

'How long should we wait for him?' Valente came over to sit with us, a little away from the small fire we had made.

'I don't think Nelita will be fit to go on in the morning,' I said. 'We'll have to wait anyway.'

She still wouldn't look at her baby, so I kept it with me. No one slept, so I don't know how we didn't hear her go, pushing aside the sleeping bag that had covered her and somehow finding the strength to drag herself away. In the creeping grey of emerging day, we saw that all she had left us of herself was her blood and the smell of her sweat on our foam bed.

And her daughter. Now there was an extra child to carry with us, but she was too little weight to be a physical burden. At every stop I would try to suckle her. She did eventually take some milk, but still she died in the red sunset, with only a small groaning sound. Ido and Valente scraped out a hole for her. I still wonder if the small rocks we used to cover her were enough, or if hyenas or jackals would have come for her later, when we had moved on.

The men were sweating and turned away quickly, but one of the other women and I stood for a minute. We didn't know what name Nelita and Pekiwa might have chosen for their daughter, so we just said a blessing.

Rolling up our bed in the morning, I felt a heaviness in myself. The discoloured foam was beginning to break in places, and a scattering of yellow crumbs looked like maize meal dusting the red-brown ground when I lifted the bed to give it to Ido.

We had to unroll it again a few hours later when the hippo got Valente while he was fetching water. For his comfort only. We couldn't save him, only listen and try to soothe his delirium.

The shape of the stain his blood left on our mattress made me think of a big palm leaf, ragged at the edges.

A kindness: the Kruger National Park is narrow, soon crossed.

The local people seemed friendly, giving us directions, when we got to the lowveld kasi where Celano lived.

'I'd given you up!' he roared in his big voice when he saw us. 'Busi, they are here! I tell you, I feared for you after you sent word and then you didn't come – how long has it taken you?'

Ido and I looked at each other.

'What day is this?' Ido asked and I understood that he too had lost count of the days during our walk.

Celano looked from Ido's face to mine. 'Too long, I can see. It went badly? But you are here now, that is the thing. And with your little one, look at him! Come, come inside.'

He helped us find materials to add on to his shack. One of the first things I did was wash our mattress. It was the same thing as before. After a while I could see only the faint outlines of stains. It felt fresh and clean, though. Almost new, to go with our new start.

We found piece-work. With a small audience of geckos, we would lie and talk about the future, but also of home.

'Home isn't so far. Just next door,' I reminded Ido.

'This is home,' he said.

It was a small difference, but I felt it like an empty space between us.

There was no empty space in our bed. We bought two pillows and a thin quilted cover from the man who sold factory rejects at the bus depot. The cover had a leopard print. Part of me hankered after a deep orange one with lots of ruching and beadwork embroidery, but Ido said it wasn't practical, especially with a child in the room.

Walking back to Celano's, Ido carried the pillows and I had the cover, with Niando on my back. As we walked, Ido grew quieter, and

I wondered what was wrong, but I didn't pay too much attention because Niando was hot and complaining.

'People don't seem so friendly any more,' Ido said when we were sitting outside with Celano and Busi that night. 'When we came home with the new things, there were – I don't know, there were some looks. As if people thought they hadn't seen us before and we had come to the wrong place.'

'It's because they see that you can buy stuff,' Busi said. 'They are jealous.'

Ido was frowning, but by the time we went to bed his usual optimism was back. I was glad. I was excited about sleeping under our new cover.

With Niando cocooned beside our bed in his nest of fleece blankets, we lay awake whispering some more about the future. Ido was ambitious, and I thought that was a good thing. He believed we should go to Nelspruit, or even Jozi.

'Are we big enough for such places?' I asked.

'We crossed The Park,' he said. 'What can frighten us now?'

'Sometimes I'm more terrified of people than of wild animals.'

'We'll watch out for each other.' He was so confident. 'Celano has contacts. He's going to find out about work for us. With full-time work we might be able to live somewhere with four real walls. We'll buy a proper bed.'

'Busi says something fell out of their marriage when they bought a big bed. Sometimes they can't find each other in the night.'

Ido laughed. I could feel his chest vibrating against my milk-full breasts.

'We'll buy a very small bed.'

I wasn't sure how I felt about parting from our strip of foam with its ghost-stains.

I said, 'There will be more competition in the big places.'

'More opportunities.'

That was the difference between us. When we were trying to come to South Africa, all those setbacks had made me think it wasn't meant to be, but Ido had been determined, and here we were.

It was a good night, even with Niando waking twice. Our new cover felt just right, light and not too warm but somehow sheltering. I thought Niando was probably too hot in his fleecy nest, so eventually I took him in with us, but in the morning I could see it was something more.

'What's that thing? Prickly heat?' That was Ido's first idea.

'I'm not sure. Ido, remember how we joked that he was growing out of being just a baby because he's not so round and fat any more? Maybe something else is making him thin?'

'The walk,' Ido spoke very fast. 'It was hard. It took the goodness out of your milk.'

But I knew it wasn't that. I was scared. Inside myself, I knew it was malaria, but I couldn't make myself say it out loud. Ido didn't want to admit it either. When Celano suggested it, he grew angry.

'It's tick-bite fever,' he insisted because that's what the nurse at the clinic had said after first thinking it was flu.

'Then why isn't the medicine working?'

We borrowed money for the bus from Celano and took Niando to the big hospital in Nelspruit. The Outpatients was the busiest place I've ever been in, with so many sick and injured people all trying to get someone's attention or needing help filling in forms and nobody sure where they were supposed to go. I don't know how many hours we waited for someone to help us, and then it was hard to understand what the people were saying.

Niando was too sick to cry when they gave him an injection. The tears were mine.

When we took him home I laid him on our bed. First I wetted his lips and then I gave him a dose of the medicine from the hospital. I saw how the smooth baby fat was beginning to melt from his cheeks, and thought bitterly of the pride I'd felt, taking it as a sign that he was growing from a baby into a little boy. His eyes stared out of his face, huge and too bright with fever.

He couldn't tolerate the cover or his blankets, fighting them with rigid arms and legs, so we let him lie there on the yellow foam.

I stared at the faint persistent outlines of stains marking it. They weren't all from life's big dramas and the fluids that leak from us at birth and death and loving. I knelt beside my child trying to identify those stains, building a wall against an emptiness I felt I must surely bring about merely by contemplating.

I'm not sure how long I knelt reading stains like a map of our lives together. Hours, yes. But a day and a night, or more? Sometimes Ido came and sat with me, or Celano would look in and go away, sombre and heavy-footed. Twice Busi brought food and drink, but I couldn't swallow, or swallowed too fast, feeling it a betrayal of our son to be eating with him the way he was.

He made the same small groaning sound as the baby that died in The Park.

I picked him up and showed him to Ido. He didn't say anything, only turned and stood with his head bent for a while. Then he walked out of the shelter. I could hear someone wailing. It was me.

After a while, Ido came back with Celano and Busi. They took Niando out of my arms and I fell face forward onto our bed, howling like some animal. I bit and tore at the foam with my teeth, and gouged at it with my fingers curled like claws.

Later I rolled onto my back and saw that even though night had come there were no geckos on the cement wall. It was our only cement wall – the windowless end of Celano's two-room shack. I often thought the pink geckos looked made of plastic, pop-eyed as they watched us through the mosquito nights, malaria nights. We would wonder to each other why they rejected the corrugated plastic and tin sides of our shelter.

After the funeral I sat trying to push pieces of foam back into the holes from which I had dug them. I noticed that there were several widening cracks in the foam, the sort of fissures you see in the ground when it is hard and dry.

I did not want to cover the foam. I did not want to turn it over, the way I usually did quite regularly. I believed I could see the imprint of Niando in the foam. How could I turn it to the dirt floor?

That night I realised how over time our weight had flattened and thinned the foam rubber. I could feel every small unevenness in the floor, but that wasn't why I couldn't sleep.

Ido stopped talking, but he held on tighter than ever before when we lay in our bed, only letting go to slap at the silent biting mosquitoes, while I worried about the buzzing ones getting in our ears.

'What about this xeno-madness thing that is happening in Gauteng?' Celano said one evening, more seriously than he spoke when he was just trying to get us to be interested in things again. 'It started in Alexandra, but it's spreading they say ...'

I couldn't make myself care, and it seemed Ido didn't want to hear, but Celano began keeping his radio on all day and half the night. We heard him telling Busi how lucky it was that we were all still here in this small lowveld kasi and not gone to Gauteng.

'We have become makwerekwere,' he said, though Busi was half-South African.

Eventually Ido paid attention. 'I don't understand it,' he said to me when we were getting ready to go to bed one night. 'When we arrived all the South Africans we met talked about being able to imagine they were us. Remember that woman who said *we are you, you are us?*'

He didn't hear the answer I started to make. As if talking about it brought it to us, an explosion of loud, confused noise swallowed the normal night sounds of many people living close together. We heard screaming and angry shouting, people running and a crackling sound we knew was fire when we saw the night outside come alive with leaping orange light.

Who decided where and how?

It seemed so random.

I couldn't grasp it. Young men came beating and burning. Even some Swazis were attacked although parts of Mpumalanga share their language. They tried to burn our things. The cover from our bed was ablaze, and beginning to blacken and melt. The bed itself simply seemed to shrink, browning at the edges. Then Ido started stamping out the burn. Blood was dripping from his nose and his hands were raw from fighting them off, young men little more than children, who had come at me.

Ido was shouting at me to take what I could and run – run and hide. Thunder boomed in my head, heavier and slower than the hammering in my chest as I ran, crouched over because now the stones were coming, thrown by more people come to join the first young men.

Terror was everywhere. People became urgent, inhuman shapes, capering or fleeing in the glare from the fires, but the shadows looked like waiting traps, too close to the flames and the leaping, chanting mob.

I was sure I would never see Ido again. After the fires were put out and the sounds of conflict had subsided, some of us who had hidden began to find each other, guided by sounds of sobbing or moans and cries of pain. Together, a group of us walked to the kasi police station to ask for shelter.

That was where Ido found us in the morning. He had our bed with him, stinking of burn and smoke. Smelling too of us, as if the heat of its burning had brought out all the old human smells. For a short time I felt ashamed. Then I thought – why must I be? Like the stains, those smells told not just of Ido and me and Niando, but of those who had walked into South Africa with us. I should be proud.

We were placed in a camp. Celano too and even Busi, because she hid her documents and said she was a foreigner so as not to be separated from Celano. For the first few days no one said or did anything. We were too stunned. We just sat and waited, wherever we were told to go. I felt sick most of the time, but that was all I felt.

The faint burnt smell of our mattress made the nausea even worse, but it was difficult enough to keep ourselves and our clothes clean in that crowded camp where we had to stand in long lines for everything, even water. Washing our bedding was impossible. I tried, rubbing over it with a wet cloth, but I only made it worse.

'Are you sure it's the bed making you sick?' Busi asked me one morning when I was worse than usual, and there was that thing in her voice and her look that forced me to think.

'There's another baby coming,' I told Ido that night, filled with rage against him.

I saw something come back that had been gone from his face since Niando died.

'You say that as if I have done something bad to you,' he said.

'That's how I feel. As if you have purposely made me pregnant to replace Niando.'

'I admit I will be glad of another child –'

'It feels disloyal. And to be waiting for a baby here in this place.' I looked around. 'This is no place to start life.'

We were traitors. Anger and guilt kept me moody all through the pregnancy.

There was talk of returning to Mozambique. Some couldn't wait to go, but Ido and Celano refused to give up their South African dream.

'When things calm down outside,' they said. 'Then we'll find a way to leave.'

The new boy was born in the afternoon. He came out in a rush, just like Niando. This time Ido was with me, but Busi was more help to me and even saved our bed from too many new stains.

Then, with the foam uncomfortably bunching up behind me in the place between my back and buttocks as I raised myself, I felt the new boy's hot mouth groping for my breast, and I stopped being angry.

'Let's call him Niando,' Ido said.

'No!'

Niando was gone. I spoke so loudly and firmly that he didn't argue with me.

'Then should we call him Celano? For all he has done for us since we came out of Mozambique. He is a good friend.'

I agreed, but in my secret mind I continued to think of him as the new boy, a loud baby with funny ways, making us laugh. That was good. Ido no longer went hours without speaking. In our bed at night we whispered about the future again, uncertain though it seemed.

Soon after the birth Celano and Busi disappeared from the camp, and I knew that Ido hoped to follow soon,

I wasn't so sure. I told myself I had to stop being so negative and pessimistic. I needed to be strong and unafraid, for Ido and me, but especially for the new boy who was bringing us both back to life. I wanted so many things for him, and this country could give them to him if we worked hard – and if we were lucky, because I've always seen that hard work alone is never enough.

So we planned in the night, and made arrangements by day, and one morning we slipped away with our child, our bed and the few other things Ido had saved when we were attacked. We came into South Africa taking turns to carry the bed on our backs, but now we pushed it in a Pick n Pay trolley. Ido made a joke about being upwardly mobile.

Last night we laid our fire-shrunken bed on the floor in the home of one of Busi's cousins. This morning, ready to resume our journey, I carried it outside. As I bundled it up to fit into the trolley, it broke in half. I looked at it and my eyes were dry but burning. I couldn't swallow or speak.

'Leave it,' Ido said, seeing what had happened.

So I did, dropping the two scarred pieces at the dusty roadside.

With our new boy on my back and Ido pushing the trolley, we set out. A movement at the edge of sight made me stop. Two stunted street children were darting forward to grasp the two pieces of foam rubber with small greedy hands.

Then I watched them run away with our broken bed, and I was glad its story would go on.

Shortlisted for the
Caine Prize | 2011

In the Spirit of McPhineas Lata

LAURI KUBUITSILE

This tale begins at the end; McPhineas Lata, the perennial bachelor who made a vocation of troubling married women, is dead. The air above Nokanyana village quivers with grief and rage, and not a small amount of joy because the troubling of married women, by its very definition, involved a lot of trouble. But, maybe because of his slippery personality, or an inordinate amount of blind luck, McPhineas Lata seemed to dodge the bulk of the trouble created by his behaviour, and left it for others to carry on, on his behalf. He had after all, admitted to Bongo and Cliff, his left and right side kicks, that troubling married women was a perfect past-time which was 'all sweet and no sweat'.

Women in the village of Nokanyana, named after a small river that no one had yet been able to discover, were notoriously greedy, and, without exception, surly. Husbands in the village were all small and thin with tight muscles worked into knots because they spent all of their lives either working to please their wives or withstanding barrages of insults and criticisms for failing to do it up to the very high expectation of Nokanyana women. For Nokanyana men, it was a lose-lose situation and, as a result, each and every one of them despised McPhineas Lata merely for remaining single – he had made the right decision and they had not.

McPhineas Lata, though thus despised by most husbands, was adored by most wives. His funeral was full of dramatic fainting and howls of grief echoing as far as the Ditlhako Hills. Tears fell by the bucketful and nearly succeeded in creating the village's missing namesake. The husbands stood at the back of the gathering wearing variations on the theme 'stern face' while the minister said his last words. When it was time to pour dirt on the coffin of McPhineas Lata, the husbands rushed past their crying wives and grabbed up the shovels. Some even came prepared with their own to make the work faster. Indeed, no one could remember a burial that had lasted for so short a time. No sooner had the wives heard that first shovel-ful of soil hit against the wooden coffin, as they were still organizing themselves for their final grand crescendo of wailing, than the soil was seen to be heaped into a great mound over the grave. The men then piled stones on top, of a great number sure to keep McPhineas Lata firmly in his eternal bed. The men stacked the shovels by the grave, slapped the soil off their hands, and led the way back to the village leaving all their McPhineas Lata problems in the cemetery for good. Or so they thought.

As the husbands made their happy ways to Ema Rengwe Bar, MmaTebogo, one of McPhineas's greatest fans, lingered behind looking longingly at McPhineas Lata's grave. She wondered how the women of Nokanyana would manage without such a talented man. She also wondered what the women would do with all of their spare time. There was only so much husband haranguing a woman could stand. She thought about how much she personally would miss McPhineas Lata and without so much as a warning her mind floated away into McPhineas Lata Land.

Naledi Huelela stopped on the thin lane leading from the cemetery to the village and looked back at McPhineas Lata's grave and spotted MmaTebogo. 'What does she think she's doing?' she asked with indignation. The wives stopped and turned to see MmaTebogo lying on top of McPhineas Lata's grave. 'She can't do that!' Naledi said. She felt quite proprietal over McPhineas Lata since he had died in her bed in the middle of one of his more gymnastically performed sessions. It really had been quite extraordinary what he could get up to. People said he read books.

'Read books?' Bongo responded with a sceptical air when asked by the husbands who had gathered at Ema Rengwe Bar after the funeral.

Though they had left the cemetery in a jovial and confidant mood, a comment by Zero Maranyane put paid to that. He had looked up from his first beer and said, 'I doubt our wives will forget him as quickly as we will.'

It was a bitter taste of what their McPhineas Lata-less future was going to hold. No, Nokanyana wives would not forget McPhineas Lata. It would have been better if he had lived to a ripe old age where his muscles and frail, old man body would have let the wives down and would have had them drifting back to their hard-done-by husbands. Instead, he died as virile as ever, for god's sake, he died in the act of one of his more acrobatic performances, or so the husbands had heard.

The husbands were in a predicament. They knew enough to realize that a dead and buried McPhineas Lata didn't mean dead and buried McPhineas Lata *memories*. Memories that would likely swirl and twirl in their wives mind, adding salt and strength until McPhineas Lata became an untouchable super-sex hero with whom they could never compare. They realized then that they had quite a problem with McPhineas Lata dead and buried. Their wives had been almost manageable when he was around, but now the husbands expected the worst.

So they grilled McPhineas Lata's left sidekick, Bongo. 'McPhineas Lata reading books? No, he was far too lazy for that. Mostly, I always put it down to a good imagination,' Bongo offered. 'Imagination?' the husbands asked. If that was the case, they were most certainly doomed.

RraTebogo stood up to address the husbands. He was in the same rudderless boat as they were, but he knew they needed a plan if there was to be any hope at all. 'Men! Men! If McPhineas Lata had imagination, why can't we get some of it? Why not? Just because we never had imagination before, doesn't mean we can't change. To be honest, I don't think we have a chance if we don't.' Then he turned to McPhineas Lata's right hand sidekick, Cliff , 'So did he ever give you any pointers? Any advice?'

Cliff, not the brightest bulb in the box, looked to Bongo for help. 'He did say once that it was good to regulate speed,' Cliff offered up as assistance. The crowd nodded in approval.

Some took out pocket-sized notebooks and wrote down the advice, but before they put a full stop on the sentence, Bongo added, 'But he said speed was also dependent on the woman's likes and dislikes.' The crowd's elation at their perceived progress fell like a lead balloon when they found they were back to the start line.

A particularly gnarled and knotty fellow named Tobias Oitlhobo-gile stood up. Hunched over, he said in a battered voice, 'Maybe we should work together to come up with McPhineas Lata's method. I don't see any of us finding it out on our own.' The husbands nodded. It was better that way, at least if they failed, which in all likelihood would be the inevitable outcome, together it wouldn't feel so personal.

And they could always meet at Ema Rengwe to commiserate; at least that would be something to look forward to.

So while the wives were fighting it out, trying to climb on top of McPhineas Lata's rocky grave to give him a few last humps, the husbands made a plan of how together they would, by the process of elimination, come up with McPhineas Lata's secret for satisfying their wives.

RraTebogo, the headmaster at the local primary school, rushed to collect a blackboard which he and Ntatemogolo Moeng carried back to the bar. They would use it to map out their plan. They knew that there were only so many things that one could do when it came to making love so they divided the work into a few main categories. The husbands had decided to work in a logical, deductive manner. They would start broadly and work down to the intricate details. All evidence collected would be brought back to Ema Rengwe, discussed, and compiled into notes by the elected secretary, Mr Mokwadi Okwadile, the local accountant. They were going to be systematic and with a good effort by everyone, they were almost assured of success.

The women trickled home from the cemetery over the next week, tired and hungry and more surly than usual. A thunderstorm on the weekend meant no woman could buck and ride on the grave as she mourned McPhineas Lata, and the men knew the time had come to begin collecting the information they needed.

RraTebogo was given the broad topic of foreplay. Once Tebogo, their son, was born almost thirty-six years previously, RraTebogo had thought as the natural course of things, foreplay should be abandoned in lieu of sleep. Reintroducing such a long forgotten activity after such a substantial period of time proved to be a bit touch and go. On his first attempt, which even he recognized later as slightly overambitious, MmaTebogo stuck her head under the covers and responded 'What the hell do you think you're doing Old Man?' Lost for words, RraTebogo rolled over and went to sleep.

The next day he decided he'd have to take things a little slower. Before getting down to business, he rubbed her right shoulder for three minutes. The time-span he knew for certain as he made sure the digital alarm clock Tebogo had bought them for Christmas was positioned at the correct angle as to be seen from the bed. Then he stroked her left side four times in sequence and then promptly proceeded with the business. Since MmaTebogo neither shouted nor hit him, he marked it up as a success and passed his news on to the others that night at Ema Rengwe.

Mokwadi looked up from his notebook, his eyes swimming behind his thick, Coke-bottle glasses. 'Was that four minutes on the shoulder and three strokes on the side?'

'No,' RraTebogo corrected. 'Three minutes on the right shoulder and four strokes of the *left* side. Don't forget that left. I might be a bit subjective, but it seemed that the left side is the right side for the stroking. Anyway, we'll know soon enough.'

And indeed they would, for once something was seen to work all of the husbands took the bit of information home and put it into practice in their beds. So for a week of nightly sessions in each and every home in Nokanyana, husbands were giving their wives three-minute rubs of the right shoulder and four strokes of the left side before getting down to the business. The wives were curiously quiet throughout the week. A few hardcores still climbed up the hill to the cemetery to cavort with the memory of McPhineas Lata, but the rest stayed at home, more confused than anything. Something strange was happening in Nokanyana and they didn't want to be up on top of McPhineas Lata's grave and miss the uncovering of all this mysterious activity.

*

Back at Ema Rengwe the husbands were in a jubilant mood. Things were going well with the foreplay. 'It is time to move on!' RraTebogo said, bringing out the heavy blackboard from the bar storeroom. 'Okay Ntatemogolo Moeng. You've been assigned breasts, any progress there?'

The husbands' eyes moved to the old man sitting on a stool in the corner. He stood up straight and repositioned his jacket, circa 1972, evidenced by the massive lapels and 4 cm by 4 cm checked pattern, red on tan. 'Thank you, Modulasetilo. I am happy to report that I have nothing at all to report.' The old man bowed slightly and repositioned himself with no small amount of effort on the tall stool.

'Well, have you tried anything?' RraTebogo asked in desperation. 'Even a negative result is helpful.' The husbands nodded their heads. They all knew that a hard smack from a big, disagreeable wife would teach them a lesson they wouldn't soon forget.

Ntatemogolo Moeng stood up again. 'Thank you Modulasetilo. Yes, I have tried a few things but they seem to have just made MmaMoeng very annoyed. She has taken to bringing a softball bat to bed, so considering my age and the fragility of my bones, I thought it best to stop along the way. It was a matter of health.' He climbed back up on the stool.

RraTebogo was annoyed. 'Bloody hell man, just tell us what you did so we all avoid it. I don't think any of us cherish the idea of getting hit in the head with a bat!'

'Thank you, Modulasetilo. I can say that it appears squeezing of breasts is a bit tricky – considering all of the patterns and rhythms and varying levels of pressure – I really didn't know where to start. And then, I know some of you more ambitious young men might even add in some mouth activity. I just didn't know where to start, honestly, so I thought since the two milk cows in my kraal seemed to accept the pattern I used on them, I started there. Sort of a milking action. But as I said, MmaMoeng didn't take kindly to that.' As he climbed back up on the high stool, the husbands let out a collective groan and shook their heads.

RraTebogo tried to be respectful of the old man's age. 'Are you saying you were milking your wife?'

Ntatemogolo stood up. 'Yes, Modulasetilo, that is exactly what I am saying, but be warned, I wouldn't advise it.' He sat back down.

RraTebogo looked at Mokwaledi. 'Did you write that down? We certainly don't want to go that route again.' He turned to the husbands. 'Does anybody have anything to report? Anything at all?' He couldn't help but sound discouraged. He knew a few shoulder squeezes and side strokes were not going to push the legend of McPhineas Lata out of the wives' minds. 'I have noticed a few of our wives have taken to drifting back to the grave in the late afternoon. We husbands are losing ground!'

RraTebogo looked around and saw nothing but a crowd of disappointed faces. 'Come on men, we need to put in more effort.' Then hesitantly, the secretary raised his hand. 'Yes, Mokwadi, do you have something for us?'

'I'm not quite sure. As you know, I was given speed as my area, but I discovered something that has nothing to do with that. I don't know if it is in order to mention it or not.'

'Give it over Man! Can't you see we're desperate here?'

'Well, I was experimenting with quite a fast speed and MmaMokwadi shifted to get a better view of the TV and I slipped off her and fell to the side. I happened to settle right next to her and since I was slightly out of breath, being not used to such high-energy activity, I was breathing hard right in her ear. Suddenly she picked up the remote and shut off the TV. As the week progressed, I added a few flicks of my tongue and kisses on her neck and I believe I'm on to something.'

The Nokanyana husbands burst into cheers. Some rushed forward and slapped the shy accountant on the back.

RraTebogo stood up to get some order. 'Okay, okay. This is only going to work if we can reproduce the moves in our own homes. Mokwadi, show us on the blackboard.' The slight man stood up and took the chalk. He quickly drew a diagram complete with arrows and times as to how the husbands should approach this new move. The house agreed it should be inserted in the routine after the shoulder rubbing and the side-stroking, and before the business. That night the Nokanyana husbands went home a happy lot. They began to believe that they actually could replicate McPhineas Lata's moves and that their wives would forget all about that dead wife-troubler.

*

MmaTebogo was at the communal tap filling her water tank when Sylvia Okwadile pushed up with her wheelbarrow loaded with two large buckets. They greeted each other and sat quietly together; Sylvia on the edge of the wheelbarrow, MmaTebogo on a turned up cement block, both nibbling at the words they wanted to say while watching the thin stream of water fall from tap to tank. 'Too bad about McPhineas Lata,' MmaTebogo started, hoping that Sylvia would pick it up and lead them to the topic filling both of their minds.

Sylvia adjusted the purple and red doek on her head, and then glanced at MmaTebogo from the corner of her eye. 'Everything fine there at home?' she asked.

'Yes,' MmaTebogo answered. 'Why do you ask?'

'Nothing unusual?' Sylvia wanted a bit more before she let her tongue wag freely.

'Well, now that you mention it.' And MmaTebogo began explaining the changes taking place in her matrimonial bed.

Sylvia listened, but like most people, she listened through ears that filtered things to be skewed in a general direction already decided by her. When MmaTebogo finished she asked, 'So is it three minutes on the right shoulder and four strokes on the left side?'

MmaTebogo's eyes widened. 'Yes! Yes! That is exactly it! Every night like clockwork. Then there are a few minutes of blowing in my ear, five to seven kisses on the neck, and then the business.'

'Aha! I knew it!' Sylvia said, jumping to her feet. She now had enough evidence to confirm what she already believed. She told MmaTebogo her theory. 'He's here ... with us. I knew he couldn't just leave like that. McPhineas Lata has taken up the bodies of our husbands. He has taken spiritual possession of the husbands of Nokanyana.'

MmaTebogo, a practical woman, said, 'Do you think so? Can that even happen?'

'Sure, why not? What else could it be?'

MmaTebogo had to agree she had no answer to that question. Maybe Sylvia was right. The two decided to call the wives to see if in their bedrooms they were experiencing the same transformation.

'It starts with three minutes on the left shoulder,' Karabo John said the next morning, at the meeting at the church at the end of the village.

'Left? Now that's an interesting twist,' MmaTebogo commented. 'Why would McPhineas Lata change things for only one of the wives?' The wives nodded their heads in agreement. It was indeed unusual. Maybe the theory was not correct after all.

But then Karabo John remembered, 'Okay, no ... you know Dimpho has a problem, he never could keep left and right straight.' The wives giggled. That was the answer then. It was true, they decided, McPhineas Lata had not left them when he died, he had only taken up residence in each of their husbands' bodies. They were so relieved. Many had wondered how they would go on without their weekly visits with McPhineas Lata and the grave humping was just not cutting it.

'Now it's even better,' Naledi Huelela added. 'Now we all get McPhineas Lata – *every night*. No more sharing!'

'He really is a wise man,' MmaTebogo said, nodding thoughtfully.

*

As the sun set in Nokanyana, husbands and wives had big, wide smiles planted firmly on their faces and deep in their hearts. Once darkness descended, they hurried off to the bedrooms, leaving children to fend for themselves; favourite television dramas were abandoned in this rush, as husbands and wives could hardly wait to discover what new between-the-sheets tricks and treats McPhineas Lata had in store for them.

Fool's Gold

TINASHE CHIDYAUSIKU

Somewhere, in a dilapidated wooden shack in the town of Mbare, a young man in his mid-twenties slowly came to wake in the semi-darkness of the early hours of morning. He enjoyed the chirping of birds as part of his luxurious dream until the thud of a heavy object, the noise coming from somewhere outside, disturbed him from his last moments of laziness. His eyes flew wide open, his heart was beating. Logic kicked in, he quickly realized he remained in the seclusion of his small space, that it was time to rise, and he groaned. His leaden limbs and clouded mind demanded more sleep, his eyes were still heavy with fatigue, but the imaginary chirping was the sign that it was time to get going.

His threadbare sheets and tattered blankets had kept him warm throughout the night. He was reluctant to get up and face the harsh world outside his door. His single spring-mattress bed provided him with a place to escape the reality that life was no easy flow, and despite how worn his bedding was, his bed was the only safe place he knew, to lay down his head, to drift to sleep. It beat sleeping outside in the naked space.

Sighing deeply, he made a decision to get up. Throwing his blankets aside, he shifted, sat upright. As his cracked feet touched the cold surface of the icy concrete floor, a chill gripped him. Goosebumps rose and spread, the man's skin looked like chicken flesh. He shivered, his yellow teeth chattered violently. Rubbing his hands together to generate warmth he rose to his feet. His eyes darted in the small space of his shack, becoming accustomed to the darkness. He moved forward and bumped into a stool he kept by his bedside. He yelped in pain. The man kept a candle on this same stool which toppled over when he stumbled into it. He went down on his knees and fumbled on the ground until he found it. All that remained of the candle was a stump now but it would serve the purpose none the less. A box of matches had also fallen to the floor and he retrieved it, struck a match and held it to the wick.

The small space was bathed in light.

In one corner was an old metal dish propped on a wooden box. Right beside it stood a five litre plastic bottle filled with water. The man poured water into the dish. It made a soft splash on the metal. He wished that he could heat up the icy water but he neither owned a stove nor had the time to build a fire outside. Time was precious.

Outside the air was cold, but fresh, and the man inhaled deeply. Filling his lungs, he exhaled slowly, strangely exhilarated. It was still dark out, but no longer pitch black. The sun was rising. The man was dressed only in a tattered grey T-shirt and faded brown shorts. His heels were badly cracked but he never went anywhere barefoot, he wore his old rubber slippers. Whenever they tore, he had always managed to piece the fragile rubber back together.

Something wet ran down the man's chin. Mucus ran freely from his nose. He blocked one nostril and blew to the ground, then wiped his face with his hand and wiped his hand across his shirt.

The pushcart lying against the shack wall was well concealed by thorn branches. As the man moved the branches, he pricked his thumb and blood seeped through the piercing. He sucked his dirty finger. He never could escape unscathed when each morning he removed the thorn branches, but that did not stop him from piling them on top of his pushcart. He believed that they deterred anyone who would want to steal from him.

An old woman who had come to the township from a homestead up north had told him the previous day that she had work for him and that he was to come early in the morning. It was in the direction of her place that the man started out. He moved with haste for it was getting lighter and soon the summer sun would be scorching hot. Mbare was coming alive with every step he was taking. Pots clanked, water was poured, there were sounds of children waking, mothers scolding, somewhere a radio was booming.

A sewerage pipe had burst in the lane he was walking in. At first the man wanted to vomit from the stench, but soon he grew accustomed to it. The city council never bothered to replace the broken pipes in this overcrowded residential area, because they would only burst again. The man walked through the putrid ooze, some of it splashing onto his legs, but he did not flinch.

The roads were marred with pot holes and the man had to twist and turn to avoid them. Soon he was sweating, and no longer cold. The house he was going to was around the corner and the man added more pace to his step. He was almost run over by a green Peugeot speeding from a blind corner. The man jumped out of the way of the old car in record time. He cursed the careless driver, then continued on his way.

The gate was locked with a rusted chain attached to a padlock. The man hoped that he was not late because old women were notable for their scolding. He did not need to be told off. He clanked the chain against the padlock and saw a curtain sway aside immediately and was reassured. He was expected and most probably the old woman was ready.

The frail looking woman came from the house and behind her followed a younger woman carrying two heavy travelling bags. Behind them came a man, probably in his mid-forties, who dragged what looked like a heavier bag than the bags the younger woman had brought out. He was panting when he got to the pushcart and looked drained.

The man immediately took over, piling the bags onto the cart. He could swear that the old woman had filled the last bag with bricks. He was fascinated with women who travelled. They always took with them full and heavy bags as if they were moving permanently, he chuckled to himself. The old woman wanted to go to Mbare Musika to board a bus. She kept on about how she looked forward to returning to her rural home in Murehwa. The fare decided, the man set off, leaving the old woman to come after him as fast as her old bones could carry her. By the time they got to the bus station, the woman was panting and cursing at the man. He looked at the old woman and his eyes rested on her feet. She wore beautiful black tennis shoes which the man coveted. He could not afford such luxuries. Each time he tried to save up for good shoes, the price shot up. It frustrated him. The only place he owned shoes was in his dreams and he thought wistfully of his bed were he would relax after his hard work at the end of the day. At that moment, he longed for the day to end so that he could go home and sleep.

However, back in the moment the man had to move on and look for more people he could carry luggage for. This was how he made a living. If he did not find customers he would go to bed hungry. At least in his dreams he could eat, but he would always wake up as hungry as ever. He did not wish this particular day to be one of those days when he would go to bed hungry.

Mbare Musika was a beehive of activity. People were streaming in from all directions. The man manoeuvred between people and buses. Before long the man found two women who needed his services. They wanted him to carry their produce to the market place to sell. He would have to travel only a short distance from the bus terminus to the market place, but he needed the money no matter how little it would be. Despite their pleading with him to reduce his fare, he stood firm and would not change his mind, saying that he had to eat as well. He lifted the heavy baskets of produce, his muscles straining under the weight. He transported eight baskets in two trips. On the first trip he carried five, on the second he carried the remaining three. He tried to be fast so that he could do more work. A bus drove past. He heard cries from behind him: 'Mukwasha zvinhu zvedu zvoparara here ...' – 'Son, should our goods perish ...'. The man grinned but did not say anything. He had to be fast. The faster he could push, the more money he would make. The man felt lucky. He believed that he would earn double from the two women.

However, when they got to the market place, the other women there ganged up on him and he was paid half of what he had expected to make. It was a disappointment. In his dreams he knew that he could persuade anyone and get what he wanted, but not in reality. He seethed with anger, he tasted the bitterness of humiliation. Like everyone else, he was simply trying to make a living.

Just at that moment his stomach sounded with hunger. He ignored the rumbling because he did not have enough money to buy anything to quieten it down. The man remembered a dream he had once had. He was eating a mountain of sadza and juicy beef stew and green vegetables, cooking oil dribbled down his chin.

It was still early. More work had yet to be done. He licked his chapped lips. His eyes darted back and forth picking out possible customers. He was not alone in this search. Others who pushed carts were doing the same. And other darting eyes were those of thieves and pick pockets, eyes trained to look for the vulnerable at the bus terminus. The man was determined to make it through the day. He would not steal.

On his way out off the market place a petite young woman walked up to him and requested his service. She asked him to carry some containers of water from the market place to a cooking site a stone's throw away. She asked how much it would be and the man quoted a figure that he felt was reasonable. The woman seemed startled, she made a move to walk away but the man stopped her and reduced his charge and the woman agreed. The man grumbled under his breath. Women were always complaining about his fares which he considered within reach of the ordinary person on the street.

Each container of water was very heavy. He asked the woman to add a few more notes to the fare they had agreed on, but she remained adamant and even threatened to withdrew her service and call on another person to carry her containers for less. The man's complaints were futile. He knew that someone else would offer to carry for her at a lower price; it was a competitive business. Despite the argument, he got a few notes from the woman. He managed to get another customer right away who wanted to have her firewood carried to her home at Mbare National.

It was noon and his stomach had given up its rumblings and gone quiet. Sticky sweat tricked down the man's back, his body was soon bathed in sweat as he continued his trips back and forth. His T-shirt stuck to his skin. His muscles ached, but he would not give up. Business was booming and rest was a luxury he could not afford until the evening. The man grew more and more exhausted but he would not give up. His body shivered slightly from hunger, he felt faint, but he had to keep on his feet. He passed a beer hall and grew envious of men who could afford to stop and sit, drink away their worries and eat meat. There was a braai stand where some were gathered, laughing and talking, their meat browning on the open fire. The aroma of cooked meat teased the man's nostrils. He went weak at his knees but he resisted the temptation to stand and stare like a beggar. He asked a passer by what the time was and was told that it was way past four o'clock. His heart sank. He had missed lunch ages ago, but he smiled and set his mind on looking forward to going back home to rest.

The man continued to work, focusing on doing as much as he could. The market and bus terminus was swarming with people, some of whom required his services and he went back and forth finding more. Well into the night, weak from the exhausting work, the man decided to head for a food stall. He told himself that he would reward himself with a mountain of sadza and steamy beef stew, like the meal of his dream, and he smiled to himself. He had to pass a public toilet to get to the food stall. The stench of stale urine came at him and he almost gagged from it. He had to eat. He needed energy to get back to his shack. The women at the stall chatted away as they cut meat and vegetables to cook. There were tripod pots on the fire and the beautiful aroma invited him to linger. His mouth watered. He smelled the fats and meat cooking. The site was crowded with a group of people and there was nowhere to sit. His feet felt as if they could give way under him any second.

The man gulped down his sadza, not steamy hot because he could not wait for the next lot which was still cooking. The sadza tasted as heavy as if it was wearing three coats. It was warm enough, but it did not live up to the dream-sadza the man had been looking forward to the whole day. His meat was almost done. It was tough meat that needed to have been on the fire for quite a bit longer. Disappointed, the man licked his fingers clean and dragged himself home.

It seemed to get darker with every step he took, and home seemed further and further away. He tried to pick up his pace but his legs were swollen from walking back and forth the whole day and he had started to limp.

At last, the man turned toward his shack amongst the other shacks. He was home. He overturned his cart and covered it with the thorn branches as quickly as he could. He did not feel the thorns pricking his flesh. Pushing open his wooden door he entered the dark space. He knew where he had left his candle and match box. He bumped into an unseen object and yelped in pain. He felt for his matches and scratched alight a match and lit the stump of candle. The small space was bathed in light and the man smiled as he turned to his bed.

Much as he wanted to jump onto it, he had to wait. His body was swathed with sweat and he had to freshen up first. Pouring water into his metal dish, he sank his worn-out bathing towel into the cool water, wrung it, then proceeded to wipe down his body, getting rid of dirt and grime.

Finally, the man limped towards his unmade bed and climbed into it. His tired limbs gave way, relaxing immediately. Covering himself up, he blew out the candle and his heavy eyelids immediately closed. The man drifted into a deep sleep and images of new tennis shoes and hot steaming sadza came to him. Deep breathing warmed the small space as the man dreamed off into the darkness.

The Outsider

ISABELLA MORRIS

In the feeble light of the bathroom Lorinda smeared the last blob of Coral Shimmer onto her lips and squeezed them together to spread the lipstick. She tiptoed down the narrow passage, so that the clickety-clack of her high heels didn't alert Pa, but when she crossed into the kitchen Pa was already sitting in his wheelchair next to the fire, the Raceform folded on the table next to him.

'You look fancy for a girl who's just going to the TAB,' he said.

Lorinda ignored him and picked up a piece of cold toast; she snapped off the crusts, spiralled honey onto the middle and handed it to Pa, then she leaned over and kissed him on the forehead, holding her breath against the suffocating smell rising from his unwashed hair.

While Pa sucked at the sticky toast, Lorinda examined the betting forms he had filled in. 'Rolling Thunder, he's an outsider Pa but I've also got a good feeling about his chances,' she said and placed her father's bets in her handbag. Then she knelt down on the cold stone floor and removed a bottle of Klipdrift from the bottom shelf of the kitchen dresser. Pa eyed the half-jack of brandy and patted her arm as she placed the bottle on the table. 'You're okay for a girl you know,' he said.

She unlatched the top half of the stable-door and stared up at the sky; the slow rolling clouds promised a spectacular storm. The fox terrier scratched against the door and Lorinda went outside and filled its bowl with fresh water from the tap that dripped into a patch of mint.

'Hey Bella, look after Pa, hey,' she said as she broke into a run towards Pa's bakkie, ignoring the animal's watery eyes.

The hectares of fields on either side of the highway were monotonous khaki blankets overhung with gravid clouds. Lorinda flicked the windscreen wiper lever when the first drops of rain splashed onto the windscreen, and reduced her speed to a cautious ten kilometres lower than the speed limit. She drove up and over the swells of the road until she saw the picnic area and pulled across from left to right; she drove on the opposite shoulder of the quiet road until she reached the desolate cluster of cement picnic furniture and a rusted garbage barrel, dry grass sprouting from the holes in the bottom.

She preferred to park the bakkie so that she was facing oncoming traffic, that way nobody could surprise her from behind. She took off her shoes and hobbled over the gravel, wincing at the pressure of the sharp stones underfoot. She unlocked the small doors of the bakkie, climbed into the back and knelt on the flatbed, its ridged metal bruising her knees. She unrolled the mattress with a deft movement and then she spread out the white cotton sheets that smelled of Spring Blossom fabric softener. She closed the flimsy yellow curtains she had made at sewing classes in Bethlehem the previous year, courtesy of one of Pa's gambling windfalls. When she was satisfied with the cosy bedroom she had created, she sprayed one squirt of Panache into the air then quickly jumped down from the back of the bakkie and closed the doors.

As she drove into town, she kept an eye on the dashboard clock, hoping that the TAB wouldn't be overcrowded; it was the end of the month and punters were usually over hopeful when their pockets were full.

Lorinda parked in a side street and pulled on her raincoat. The TAB was busy; punters pencilled in their choices for jackpots and place accumulators and tri-fectas as they stood in a queue that meandered drunkenly around the block. Lorinda flicked open her umbrella. It wasn't necessary; the pavement was sheltered by an over-hang, but the umbrella kept a circle of space around her. She was careful to keep her eyes downcast so that she didn't have to acknowl-edge anyone she might recognise from church or the Vroue Federasie.

Mr Kletz held out both his hands when Lorinda reached the counter; she handed the bets over to him and watched as he fed them into the machine. He kept his left hand outstretched, but Lorinda waited until the machine had finished grinding and only when she saw the red figures blinking on the small screen did she part with the money, mentally calculating her change while the machine spat out the printed tickets.

'Pretty Tart,' Mr Kletz said.

'I beg your pardon?' Lorinda asked; her armpits prickled.

'That Rolling Thunder's an outsider; a safer bet would have been Pretty Tart,' he said, but his impatient eyes had already flicked past Lorinda, and his hands were reaching to take the next punter's bets.

Back in the familiar confines of the bakkie, Lorinda accelerated, freeing herself from the town with its narrow streets and inquiring eyes. Lightning momentarily brightened the overcast sky and Lorinda wondered how many hitch-hikers were likely to be thumbing a ride in such inclement weather. She drove the bakkie to the stony ridge that formed the southern boundary of the blind Widow Verster's farm and waited there. She had to turn on the ignition every few min-utes so that the windscreen wiper could clear the raindrops. Through

Pa's old racing binoculars she could see the main road and the place where the swinging Ry Veilig / Ride Safe sign caught the light as it swayed in the storm. She'd easily see any army guys who arrived there hoping to hitch a ride to the station.

Popcorn white lambs gambolled in the fields even though it was drizzling. From the windy outcrop Lorinda watched as a corpulent Bedford truck stopped on the main road, dropped off a troepie, then made a wide circle and proceeded back up the road towards the army base.

The guy who had been dropped off was tall, so tall that Lorinda almost drove past him. She couldn't imagine his long legs finding a comfortable position in the confinement of the cab. Instead, she slowed onto the newly tarred shoulder of the road and stopped. The Ride Safe sign cast a long shadow across the bonnet. He bent down and looked at her through the window, a cautious smile; she flipped the lock.

All night long the guys had teased him about the toothless farmers who liked to pick up army guys and give them blowjobs. He had considered walking all the way to Bethlehem, but soon changed his mind when the Bedford dropped him off on the tarred road and through the light rainfall he saw nothing but a basket weave of farmlands stretching into the horizon. The driver was no farmer; she had a tight white smile and a short skirt.

'Where you going?' She asked as he squeezed himself into the bakkie.

'To Joburg.'

'How long is your leave?'

'Three days, I've got to be back on Tuesday.'

'Are you going to hitch or take the train?'

'Haven't thought that far ahead, I just wanted to get the fuck out of that shithole – sorry – for swearing.'

She couldn't decide if he was handsome in an ugly way, or ugly in a handsome way; it was hard to gauge the level of attractiveness of these bald army guys; he had bluish lips and a skein of scars, but his mouth looked kind; she would bet money that his nipples were brown instead of pink.

'Do you want to drive?' she asked him. If she spoke in simple sentences, she would manage the English.

He hadn't been behind the wheel of a car for ages, but before he could respond she reached her left hand across his lap and lifted herself over him, making sure that her bottom grazed his crotch. He could smell the apple scent of her shampoo, feel the honey heaviness of her hair against his cheek; he slid across, the steering wheel was warm where she had held it. She sat with her back against the door and tucked her right leg under her butt so that a small triangular window opened at her thighs and skirt hem and gave him a seductive view of her crotch. He started the bakkie and pulled onto the road without even looking in the mirror. It had been a long time since he had driven a car; it was even longer since he'd had screwed anyone.

As they drove towards Bethlehem the wind cracked against the bakkie, rapid as an R1 round. Platoons of poplars, match-skinny, stood to attention on the roadside.

She said, 'Are you married?'

He shook his head.

' – verloof, um, engaged?'

Another head shake.

' – gay?'

He laughed, so she did too.

She waited for him to ask her something; she wanted to tell him about herself. The other guys always asked – where she lived, who she lived with, why she wasn't married – a looker like her. But he wasn't going to ask her any of that, she could just tell from the way his eyes didn't rise quite high enough to meet hers. His disinterest left her with the same cheated feeling she got when she bought hertzoggies that had been baked with margarine instead of butter.

'I don't care if you are married or you a moffie you know – it doesn't matter to me.'

He kept his eyes on the road. Farmhouses peeped shyly from between tree-breaks, or turned their backs to the winds of the open plains.

'Are you hungry?'

He glanced across the cab as she opened the cubbyhole, shrugged his shoulders.

'Pepper-steak pie or Simba crisps – salt and vinegar flavour?' she asked.

The pie, I'll have the pie thanks.'

She slid the pie halfway out of the packet and then twisted the paper so that he could eat it without a crumb-fallout in his lap; Pa said a girl had to be clever no matter what, but it was Ma who used to say a way to a man's heart was through his stomach.

He ate the pie, using his knees to help him steer. The distance marker indicated that Bethlehem was 7km away; he kept his eyes on the road.

She leaned over and ran her fingers across the black letters of his nametag: YFOUCHARD. No space between the initials and his surname, but she had no difficulty identifying which was which.

'Yakob? Yitzhak? Yonatan? – *Jislaaik*! Are you Jewish?'

He shook his head and made the sign of the cross.

She rolled her eyes, there was only one thing Pa hated more than Jews, and that was Catholics.

'Yvan! That's it, hey? You're a Russian, or from Poland!' She bounced up and down on the narrow seat and clapped her hands.

He wasn't going to tell her his name was Yves; he despised the ignorance about his French name.

She pouted. 'You're not very friendly are you; especially considering I've just given you a lift,' she said and lifted her left leg onto the dashboard; Maybe he didn't have a lot to say, but she saw him look, his dark-lidded eyes unsettled her.

'You didn't just happen to be on the road back there, did you?' he said, slowing the car down.

She chewed at a hangnail.

'What were you doing back there, hanging around in the middle of nowhere?' he insisted.

In the early days of her courier service she had prepared excuses – like folded love-letters tucked into her mind and ready to go. 'I've got to check on one of our sick lambs at the vet in town,' or 'I got lost looking for a farm that has a foal for sale.' But army guys didn't seem to care, they were just grateful for the lift. She pretended not to understand Yves's question, instead she leaned forward, touched the blue shadow on his chin where the black stubble would break through by nightfall.

'I pick up troepies and I fuck them. Please tell me you've just come back from the Caprivi. Please, please, please! I haven't fucked anyone who's been to the border yet,' she said.

He ignored her irritating bouncing on the seat, her shining eyes. He pretended not to understand her desperation for a troepie who'd been to the border. His bunk-mate Venter had slapped his thighs with frustration when Yves told him he was heading home for the weekend pass. 'Ag, jirre, you lucky fucking poes! You know how chicks dig ou's from the border; I don't know what it is. It's like they think you got a dick like a rocket or something, fuck man!'

She edged closer to him and one by one she removed his left hand fingers from the steering wheel, she brought his hand over to her and slid his fingers into the soft place beneath her panties.

He stared at her small pointy chin, her fine narrow nose, but her eyes were closed, her head dropped back so that all he could see was taptapping in the vein that crossed the hollow of her throat.

'You can stop about two kilometres before town. There's a group of blue gums and a road that goes nowhere,' she said.

He didn't have to move his fingers; she manipulated her pelvis so that he could feel her contracting against them. It was difficult to steer and change gears with his right hand and he eventually screeched up the muddy road in first gear; she leaned over and cut the engine, his fingers twisting inside her as she did so. Then she lifted herself, disconnecting. She slid open the rectangular window hatch behind her in the cab and wriggled into the back of the bakkie. He watched her pale legs disappear. He sat in the cab for a long time listening to the wind rustling the dry leaves of the blue gums. He glanced at the window and knew he could not manoeuvre himself through the same narrow space that the girl had. He stepped out of the cab and walked around to the back. As soon as he opened the squeaky doors he smelled the fresh linen; he sat on the flatbed and unlaced his muddy boots.

She knew that if she wanted more than a wham-bam-thank-you-mam quickie she'd better get him into the mood to play for a little bit longer. Instead of stripping down completely she wore a white lace bra and panties. Her brother Rudolf's Scope said that apricot or pink underwear wasn't as big a turn-on for men as women believed it to be; black was provocative and so was red, but white was the colour that really got men's guns loaded. White was virginal, pure, and every man wanted to think he was the first, even if he knew he wasn't. By the look on his face, he was definitely pleased with her lingerie.

'My name is ...' she began, but he clamped his hand over her smile. 'It's just a fuck,' he said.

She was good at releasing khaki buttons from stiff buttonholes with her teeth; loved rolling her tongue across broad chests, but he kept her on her back by fastening her left arm behind her head in a strong grip. He was on top of her. She swallowed the lump in her throat, she had never fucked anyone whose name she didn't know. His feet were freezing. Her nipples tightened. She touched herself with her right hand and drew her fingers up to his lips but he turned away. She felt shame searing her cheeks.

When he was finished, he rolled off her and lay panting with his eyes closed. She edged closer until her face was against his shoulder; she was right, his nipples were brown with the smallest curls of dark hair around them. She could have leaned across him right then and nibbled one, but instead she closed her eyes to stop the tears. He used his feet to find his pants. He lit a Chesterfield in the back of the bakkie, blowing smoke rings so perfect she couldn't resist stabbing her finger into them. He offered her a drag but she shook her head even though she smoked a box of twenty a day. When her breath was steady enough to reassure her that she wasn't going to cry, she sat up and opened one of the small curtains. The wheat fields all around whispered a sigh of sameness that resonated so deeply within her that she knew she could not go home.

'Come with me to the cheese festival,' she said.

He kept his eyes on the ceiling; made no acknowledgement of her suggestion. Though he thought then of his parents ... He glanced at his watch – quarter to twelve, Saturday. They would be standing in Sandro's Deli, arguing over whether to buy the Ementhaler or the Edam. They would hand over the money with a grimace of reluctance because they didn't like Sandro, the Italian owner, but where else in Johannesburg were discerning French ex-pats supposed to buy quality food? Grandpère Fouchard would be in the family's pale blue Renault tapping his knees and watching the parking meter.

'Do you like it here?' she asked.

He shrugged, looked at her.

'How long have you been at this camp?'

He looked away again, drew on his cigarette.

'Give me a drag of your smoke.' She held out her fingers but he narrowed his eyes and drew on the cigarette, allowing the hot edge to run down the cigarette until it almost reached the filter, and then he blew out the thinnest reed of white smoke. 'Please come with me to the festival,' she said. She kept her eyes on her panties as she untwisted them and pulled them over her calves; they caught slightly at the damp part at the top of her thighs.

He stood next to the bakkie in his underpants and ground out his cigarette next to the rear wheel. When Maman and Papa finished their shopping they would drive Grandpère to Alliance Française where he played boules every Saturday afternoon with other old men who smelled of unwashed wool, and onions and red wine.

He took a slash against the blue gum tree. His brother Gregoire, or Greg as his friends called him, would be watching the 1st XI at the school field, and in between changeovers and innings, Gregoire would tell everyone how his brother from the border was coming home for the weekend. Surrounded by his team-mates, Greg would promise them a story on Monday – a war story, a hero's story; a story that Yves couldn't produce. Yves pulled up his zip with a violent yank and stalked towards Lorinda. 'Where would we stay?'

His question startled her. She hadn't expected an answer and was lost in her hopes that Pa's bets on Random Excuse were going to pay off. She watched YFOUCHARD pull on his khaki fatigues. She waved her hand around the bakkie, 'Ag, ons kan –'

He glanced at her sharply.

'We'll book into a caravan park; it's cheap,' she said and her hands moved quickly, snapping her lacy bra behind her, pulling on the tube of skirt and a soft white T-shirt; she didn't want him to change his mind; she tossed him the keys. 'Come, let's go.'

She turned on the radio and leaned closer to the dashboard so that she could hear the commentator. 'And it's Leaping Star and Pretty Tart. Rolling Thunder's coming up on the inside, with two hundred metres to go it's anyone's race. Habib's encouraging Leaping Star but it's Rolling Thunder making the home straight his own. Pretty Tart's not prepared to let Rolling Thunder take the race, she's holding the pace. With fifty metres to go it's Pretty Tart and Rolling Th under. Leaping Star will have to be content with a third. There's nothing between Pretty Tart and the outsider Rolling Thunder but as they cross the finish line it's –'

He leaned across her and turned down the volume.

She turned to face him, her face twisted with frustration. What would she tell Pa? But he didn't notice, he was looking in the rear-view mirror, reversing the bakkie. When they pulled onto the main road he looked at her and asked, 'What's your name?'

Heaven (or Something Like It)

SARAH LOTZ

Adele opened her eyes and stared up at the familiar banana-shaped stain on the ceiling above her bed. Idly wondering if she should ask Manu, the caretaker, to take a look at the grubby paintwork, it struck her in a moment of startling clarity that this would be pointless, as she was, in fact, quite dead. She even had a hazy recollection of the moment of her death, which had unfortunately occurred halfway through the finale of *Survivor: Antarctica*. She might never find out who'd won the million dollar prize now. She hoped it was the wimpy guy with the postadolescent acne and not the brittle blonde with plastic breasts. She'd always had a bit of a thing for the underdog.

She was less certain why it was that her soul had arrived back at her flat instead of staking a place in heaven, hell or Nirvana (or any other mythical place for that matter), but here she was, nonetheless. And although she'd been plagued by anxiety attacks most of her life, strangely enough the knowledge that she was dead didn't seem to worry her in the slightest, (although surely dying was among the top ten stressors of everyday life, after divorce but before moving house?). Oh well, it could be worse. Her bed, after all, was her refuge, the centre of her existence – she'd set it up that way. The widescreen television was conveniently fixed in place at the foot of the bed, and the two side tables that flanked the headboard were large enough to hold several hours' worth of Pringle tubes, Pepsi Max bottles and Woolworths' tikka chicken bites.

But why *had* she come back? Was she having her own personal Patrick Swayze *Ghost* moment? Could she be a restless spirit? Unlikely. She'd never been very active when she was alive. She ran her hands over her body. She certainly didn't feel ghost-like or ethereal. Dying was obviously as ineffective a method for losing excess kilos as the miracle weight-loss remedies she'd bought from Verimark infomercials.

According to the green digital numbers on the DVD player, it was 9.30am. In her old life – the one where she was actually alive – she'd be at the office by now, but there was hardly any point calling in sick in her current condition. She sat up, stretched, and looked around. The room was much the same as she'd left it, maybe a touch tidier. She sniffed the air. No scent of decay. They must have found her body fairly soon after she'd died. Probably thanks to Previn, the office manager, who was always one to sound the alarm if shirking was suspected. She was quite content to stay in bed while she figured out what to do next.

How long had she been gone? Hours? Days? Weeks? But what did it matter? There was nothing she could do about it now. She pushed all the unanswered questions out of her mind, settled back with a sigh of contentment, and reached for the remote. She flicked straight to the Series channel. *Desperate Housewives*. Lovely. She'd always felt an affinity for Lynette, the least glamorous of the women on the show, and it was her favourite episode – the one where Lynette beats cancer. Could life (or death) get better than this?

Although she could have quite happily spent the morning lost in a BBC Lifestyle *Spendaholics* marathon, the next day she decided it was time to experiment with her new 'self'. She half expected that she wouldn't be able to leave the flat, like Geena Davis in *Beetlejuice*, but it was a simple matter to slip through the door (quite literally – apparently the dead have no use for handles). She didn't bother with the lift, and cruised eff ortlessly down the six flights of stairs. Robert the security guard didn't even glance up from his *Cape Times* when she approached the front desk, nor did he react when she jumped up and down in front of him like a demented overweight cheerleader. Interestingly, though, he did flinch when she stroked her fingernails across his forearm.

A brief tour around the Garden Centre's Woolworths confirmed her suspicion that the living were as oblivious to her presence as a rich suburbanite to a squatter, and she headed gratefully back to her flat. The fact that she was invisible to those around her was nothing new. She'd never enjoyed going out or socialising, so why should this change now she was dead?

In fact, being dead had massive benefits. Death was an excellent reason to quit her job, and all her bodily functions seemed to have fled along with her pulse. She no longer needed (or felt the need) to eat, defecate, drink or wash, and consequently had no reason to leave the flat. Peculiarly, although most objects seemed to slip through her fingers, her most essential possession – the DSTV remote – responded perfectly to her touch.

*

Two weeks went by: Two blissful weeks of *Ellen*, true crime documentaries, Lifestyle programmes and Hallmark channel weepies. By the end of the second week she knew everything there was to know about the Lockerbie disaster, could have rearranged her closets with ease and she even had a fair idea, thanks to a flamboyantly gay designer type, *How to Look Good Naked* (not that this would be of any use to her in the foreseeable future). Then, one morning, as she was settling down under the covers for a movie about a woman with alopecia, she heard the unmistakable scratch of a key at the lock. The door opened, and her sister, Liza, strode into the room, picking her way across the parquet on designer wedge heels. Adele was aghast. She hadn't seen or spoken to Liza in at least five years. What on earth was she doing here?

'So this is it,' Liza said, flapping her hand in front of her face as if she smelled something foul. A youngish guy in a shiny silk suit followed her into the centre of the room. Adele couldn't take her eyes off his hair. It looked solid, almost as if it had been carved out of plastic. He had to be an estate agent. With that hair he could hardly be anything else.

'Hello, Liza!' Adele said clearly. 'Long time no see!' Neither Liza nor Plastic Hair even glanced in her direction.

'Tiny, isn't it?' Liza said. 'A what-do-you-call-it – a bachelor flat?'

Plastic Hair flashed his bleached teeth. 'We call them studio apartments.'

'Still. One room. Imagine.'

He motioned towards the bed. 'Is this where –?'

'She died? Yeah.'

'I'm sorry.'

'Don't be. We weren't close.'

Adele winced at her sister's callousness, although she had to agree with her. It was hard to believe they were even related. Adele was well-padded and phlegmatic, while Liza was high-strung and skinny. Liza's three marriages had produced four private school kids, whereas Adele's one short engagement had ended in an embarrassing sexual episode. She vaguely recalled that Liza lived in Sandton with an ANC politician, and for all intents and purposes Adele was married to her Sealy Posturpedic and DSTV remote.

'Nice big bed,' Plastic Hair said suggestively. Liza ignored him. He clearly didn't feature on her radar of possible liaisons.

'You know,' the guy said, taking Liza's dismissal in his stride. 'With the World Cup coming up, renting might be the way to go.'

'I was actually looking for a quick sale.'

Plastic Hair thrust out his chest and ran a hand over his head. His hair didn't budge an inch. 'Market's depressed. Short-term lets, holiday accommodation, that kind of thing. Could bring in a mint.'

Liza finished trailing a talon across Adele's DVD rack, and stalked over to the wardrobe to clack through the clothes.

'Look at all this!' Liza said, pulling out a rayon blouse that Adele used to wear every Wednesday to work. 'I wouldn't be seen dead in this stuff.' She glanced at Plastic Hair and they shared a collusive chuckle.

'We could rent it fully furnished,' Plastic Hair said.

'Fine. It's not as though it matters if anything gets damaged.'

'You happy to leave the television here?'

Adele held her breath, but Liza nodded as if she couldn't care less. 'Piece of junk. Why not?'

For the first time since she'd died, Adele found herself infused with emotion – anger. Piece of junk? She'd spent eighteen months paying that off. Was Liza blind? It was a Samsung for God sakes! And what right did Liza have to barge in here and sell her flat from under her? She wasn't finished with it yet! Before she was fully aware of what she was doing, Adele stalked over to where Liza was gingerly picking through her underwear drawer, grimacing at a pair of support knickers, and slapped her across the face. Although Adele felt her hand connect with her sister's powdery cheek, Liza didn't flinch, although she did drop the underpants immediately back into the drawer, where they concealed the half-empty packets of Diazepam.

'Bit chilly in here, isn't it?' Liza said. 'Cape Town winters. Ugh.' She shuddered. 'Rental it is then.'

And with that Liza and Plastic Hair left.

Two days later Adele watched from her perch on the bed as her beloved collection of Julia Roberts and Meg Ryan DVDs, Jodi Picoult novels and comfortable winter sweat suits were carelessly shoved into boxes by a crew of taciturn removal men. She didn't bother to stop them. All she needed was the bed and the television, and those were staying.

*

Three weeks later the tenants started to dribble in. Her biggest concern was the sleeping arrangements. She didn't see why she should have to vacate the bed, it was hers after all. So when the first visitor, a German businessman with pockmarked greyish skin arrived, Adele stubbornly refused to budge from her spot closest to the window. She was taken aback when he wasted no time in ringing up an escort agency, but she needn't have worried. His particular brand of fun didn't involve the bed, and in any case Adele was glued to the *American Idol* Miami auditions, and barely took any notice of the antics going on in the bathroom. After the exhausted escort left, Adele watched nervously as the German stripped down to his threadbare jocks and climbed into bed beside her. She lay with her hands tucked into her sides, rigid as a two-day-old corpse, but the guy seemed to edge as far away from her side of the bed as he could, even in his sleep. At three am he woke up shivering almost uncontrollably. Adele was pretty sure this was down to her, although she'd always thought of herself as a warm-hearted person. The next morning he packed up his briefcase and left, barking broken English expletives into his phone.

Over the next few weeks, Adele found herself sharing her space with a wide variety of single holidaymakers, businessmen and young couples seeking budget accommodation. She didn't find them too much of a pain on the whole. The main inconvenience was the lack of control over the television. Several had terrible taste in programming. One couple in particular were irrevocably hooked on E! Entertainment, a channel Adele found banal to the point of tears. She couldn't bear programmes with no narrative thread, even *Oprah*, *Hell's Kitchen* and *The Amazing Race* had something of a story-line if you looked closely enough.

It was the male tenants who generally had the worst taste. Although they didn't watch quite as much sport as she'd feared, more than one had flicked onto e-TV for the late night 'erotic selection' while fumbling lamely under the covers. Any regrets Adele might previously have harboured about being single were snuffed out after sharing her bed with several choice specimens. It was incredible how many of them would grunt, fart, moan and scratch in their sleep. The couples were almost as bad. Adele had assumed that she'd be sidelined during torrid sex sessions, but this wasn't the case. Most preferred to expend their energy sniping at each other. And hiding the remote didn't seem to help. The more resourceful of them figured out that channels could be changed on the television itself. She had one notable battle of wills with an elderly Joburg businessman when her finale of *The Bachelor: London Calling* clashed with *Top Gear*. She'd been forced to run her fingers over the businessman's sweaty pate to eject him out of the flat, but it had been worth it. She loathed Jeremy Clarkson.

After a while Adele grew used to the sound of Plastic Hair's voice as he wearily introduced another unfortunate tenant to the flat. But they never stayed longer than two days before hastily packing up and heading to the nearest Formula One. From the furious cell phone calls they made as they fled, most of them were seriously freaked out by the flat's 'vibe'. In particular, they objected to the 'haunted television' that would mysteriously channel hop at night, and that would switch itself on, even when the flat was deserted.

Gradually fewer and fewer lessees arrived to disrupt Adele's peace, and she found herself drifting back into her routine of cruising the light entertainment channels. She didn't miss the interruptions, and began to feel a curious and passionate kinship with the inhabitants of Albert Square, Wisteria Lane and the Baltimore gangsters of *The Wire*. They were her family. She didn't need anyone else.

*

Then, one rainy Tuesday morning, as Adele was snuggling in to watch *The Bold and the Beautiful* followed by a two-hour made for television movie about a rapist, she heard the tell-tale scrabble at the lock and the sound of muffled voices. She recognised Plastic Hair's nasal tones instantly. He marched into the room, a woman trailing in his wake. This was a first. Adele had shared her flat with several men of all ages and at least five couples, but never a woman on her own. Adele eyed her with interest. The woman appeared to be about her age, overweight (but on the right side of obese), and clearly uncomfortable in her own skin. She continually tugged at the hem of her over-sized T-shirt, stretching it to cover her bum. Adele felt a sudden rush of what she could only call 'sisterliness' for her. She wished she could tell her that dying was great for self-consciousness and other body-image issues.

'So this is it,' Plastic Hair said, not even bothering to sound fakely enthusiastic. Despite herself Adele felt slightly sorry for him. His failure to secure even a temporary tenant must be taking its toll. And failure was something Adele understood perfectly. Plastic Hair peered at the television and scrunched up his nose in irritation. 'Not again.'

He strode towards the bed and snatched at the controller, brushing against Adele in the process. He paused, shivered then tried to hide his discomfort with a nervous cough and a glance in the mirror on the wall in front of him.

The woman remained silent and shuffled towards the window to check out the view over Hope Street.

Behind her back Plastic Hair smothered a yawn. 'I think I should tell you,' he said, scuffing his pointy black shoes on the parquet flooring, 'We've had a few ... complaints about the flat.'

'Oh yes?'

'People say that they feel ... strange when they're in here.'

'What do you mean?' The woman sat down on the bed and bounced gently on the mattress. Adele moved with her. It wasn't an unpleasant feeling.

He tried to laugh, but it sounded forced. 'You know, they say crazy things – that it's haunted, that kind of thing. Ridiculous really.'

'Oh. That kind of thing doesn't bother me,' the woman said.

'I wouldn't have said anything, only ... if you took a long lease ... once you'd signed it would be tricky to get out of it.'

'That's fine. Really.'

Plastic Hair looked annoyed that she wasn't hanging onto his every word. He leaned towards her. 'She committed suicide, you know,' he murmured. 'The woman who lived here. The woman who owned this flat.'

Adele sat up. 'I didn't!' she shouted, indignant. How dare he lie like that! For a second she forgot that she couldn't be heard. For some reason it was suddenly very important to her that the woman know the truth about her death. Adele flopped back down on the bed. But what was the truth? How *had* she actually died? She'd assumed it was some sort of embolism brought on by too many Woolworths' steak and kidney pies. Her recollection of the exact moment of her death was vague at best. But in the scheme of things, what did it matter? Dying had turned out to be the best thing that had happened to her in her whole life.

Plastic Hair coughed impatiently. 'So what do you say? Interested?'

'I'd like a long lease,' the woman said. 'Will that be a problem?'

*

The woman – Carmen (according to the *Dish* magazine envelope) – moved in two weeks later. Adele didn't think the woman's name suited her, but then she'd always thought her own name was equally incongruous – more suitable for a French schoolgirl than a middle-aged woman. Adele watched with interest as Carmen methodically unpacked her few possessions. On the whole she approved. Carmen had quite a comprehensive DVD collection, many of them duplicating Adele's own favourites. How lovely, she thought, eyeing *Pretty Woman* and *Don't Look Now*. She was dying to see those again!

That night, when Carmen climbed into bed, Adele reached over and softly touched her hair. Carmen froze for a second, then simply shook her head, turned over and fell asleep, considerately leaving the television tuned to the Crime and Investigation channel. Adele was flummoxed. She'd never encountered that reaction before. No matter. Tomorrow was another day.

The next afternoon, Adele made sure the television was on at maximum volume when Carmen returned home from work. But instead of tutting in irritation and reaching for the remote, Carmen merely paused at the door, shrugged and started to unpack her groceries. Curiouser and curiouser. Carmen didn't seem to be even slightly perturbed at her dead housemate's behaviour. In fact, over the next couple of days, it was almost as if she was encouraging Adele's antics. Carmen would let whatever movie, talk show or reality sound-bite Adele had left on run its course while she made her supper, selected that evening's snacks and got ready for bed.

As the days rolled on, it became clear that their taste in television was uncannily similar. Sometimes Adele even forgot that Carmen had control of the remote when she was home – it was as if they shared a psychic connection when it came to changing channels. Carmen would inevitably nip a tedious serial killer documentary in the bud at the exact point where Adele herself would have done so. And only last night Carmen had switched from a re-run of *The Office* to *Love, Actually* just as Adele was thinking she was in the mood for a light romantic comedy.

By the end of the first week, Adele actually found herself looking forward to Carmen's return home from work. She'd often spend the hour just before Carmen was due to arrive cruising the channels for something her new housemate might like to watch. Soon she could tell by the sound of Carmen's footsteps as she approached the door if it was a *Strictly Come Dancing* night (bad day at work), or a documentary on Arthur Shawcross (pre-menstrual cramps). Life soon found a peaceful rhythm, and they were rarely interrupted. Like Adele when she was alive, Carmen seldom left the flat, and she hadn't received a single visitor since she moved in.

Until one Friday evening. Adele and Carmen were lying in their usual places on the bed. *Project Runway* was on, and they were watching with bated breath as a wiry Israeli designer burst into tears as his fabric 'misbehaved'. Both women jumped as the intercom buzzed. Adele didn't miss the look of dismay on Carmen's face.

There was the brisk clitter-clatter of heels from the corridor outside, a sharp rat-tat-tat and Carmen opened the door to a slender woman who could have played the role of a brittle DA in *Law and Order: Special Victims Unit*. The woman kissed the air around Carmen's hair, then triptrapped over to the couch. She perched on one corner, a fixed smile on her face.

'This is ... homely, Carmen!'

Carmen seemed to shrink into herself, as if her already limited selfesteem was dribbling out of a leak in her skin.

The woman sighed and nodded towards the television. 'Please turn that off. You're not a child who has to watch television continuously, are you?'

Was it Adele's imagination, or did Carmen glance apologetically towards her side of the bed as she reached for the remote?

'That's better.' Adele could see that the woman meant business. 'Now. You know Mom's not getting any younger.'

Carmen looked down at her hands. 'I know.'

'Not to mention her other problems. The forgetting, the wandering. That sort of thing.'

Head still bent, Carmen picked at the skin around her thumbnail. Adele hardly recognised her as the same woman who could watch a documentary on Jeffrey Dahmer without wincing at the gushy bits.

'Now. Grant and I have been discussing it, and we've decided that it's only fair that you should be the one to move back in with her.'

Adele watched, fascinated, as Carmen's head snapped up. Even from her perch on the bed, she could make out the glitter of tears in Carmen's eyes. She'd only seen her housemate cry once, during a particularly emotionally trying episode of *Grey's Anatomy*.

'Why me?' Carmen said, voice wavering. 'You're her favourite!'

The woman sighed. 'Yes. But I have a family. I couldn't possibly –'

'I have a life!'

'You go girl!' Adele said, recalling a similar conversation from her own life. But she didn't want to dwell on how that had turned out.

'Come on, Carmen. You can't call this a life! This place is ... is ... squalid! What kind of a life could you possibly have?'

'I have my job!'

'You hate your job! You've told me that countless times. If you moved in with Mom you'd be far more comfortable.'

'Why not put her in a home?'

'Have you any idea how much they cost?'

'But she hates me!'

'No she doesn't!'

Adele was leaning so far forward that she almost slipped off the bed.

'She does! You know she does!'

The woman sighed, stood up, brushed at the back of her skirt as if sitting on the couch had soiled it somehow, and stalked towards the window. She pulled the curtain aside and gazed down into Hope Street. 'You don't want to live like this at your age! It's ridiculous.'

Adele watched as a tear wobbled down Carmen's right cheek.

The woman rolled her eyes and, as Adele had hoped she would, sat down on the bed. 'Really, Carmen. You're becoming an embarrassment to the family.'

'I just want to be left alone!'

Now that was a sentiment Adele understood. Taking a deep breath, she pulled her legs underneath her body and launched herself at the woman, smothering her in a bear-hug. Adele could smell the powder on her skin and the greasy scent of her lipstick.

The woman froze. She remained immobile for less than a second, and then she pushed herself off the bed with the suddenness of someone experiencing an electric shock. She skittered over to the kitchenette and leaned against the counter, eyes bulging. But Adele wasn't finished with her. She glided over and traced her fingertips over the woman's forearms. The woman jumped and immediately began brushing herself down as if her skin was writhing with invisible spiders.

Adele checked Carmen's reaction. She was still sitting on the couch, staring straight at her sister, who had finally found her voice.

'Ugh!' she said. 'Ugh!' But it seemed that was all she could manage. With a final terrified glance around the room she grabbed her handbag and fled, high heels scoring tiny circles in the parquet.

Adele settled herself down on the bed and waited to see what would happen next.

Carmen remained motionless until the click-clack of running high heels was no longer audible from the corridor outside. Then she stood up, wiped a hand across her damp eyes, and walked over to the bed.

For a second Adele was certain that she looked directly into her eyes.

'Thank you,' Carmen whispered, before climbing into bed and clicking back to *Project Runway*.

They were just in time to catch the climax. Both mouthed 'Auf Wiedersehen' in unison with Heidi Klum as the Israeli designer made a tearful departure, and at the exact same moment their hands found the remote and flicked over to *So You Think You Can Dance*.

Maybe, Adele thought, as she settled back into her pillow next to her friend, this was heaven, after all.

Spying

COLLEEN HIGGS

I bumped into your folks at the Hypermarket the other day. I hadn't
thought much about you in years. They were buying a ladder and a
new washing machine. It was such a shock to see them after all this
time. They still look exactly the same, just older. Where does your
old lady buy her dresses? I have never seen dresses like that except at
a shop in Parkhurst in the 70s. Geraldine Gowns. She said you're
still in London, got a kid now and all. Seeing them like that set me
thinking about you and about us.

Do you remember the time I spied on you? You knew I was there,
but not till you got to the parking lot. You recognized my old Toyota
bakkie. You were furious and I can't say I blame you. I'm surprised
Diane didn't notice the bakkie too. Perhaps she did, but she didn't
say anything. You'd have mentioned that when we spoke on the phone
later and you gave me hell. Even months after we split up you still
told me all kinds of stuff about her that you shouldn't have, like how
she was on the pill. Later on I realized that the word stalking applied
to me. Not that I made a big habit of it or anything. The two of you
had been to a movie, at Rosebank. I saw you riding up the escalator
holding hands. You a bit taller than her, your straight dark hair a
stark contrast to her long wavy blonde hair, your face relaxed, looking
down at her as she spoke. She was wearing a loose cotton dress in
two shades of lime green, and slip slops. I was sitting at that coffee

shop at the top of the escalators drinking rooibos tea, my heart beating too fast already for coffee. She looked like a school girl version of a Botticelli Venus.

I'd worked it all out, we had been talking about movies, and you told me that you were planning to see a movie at the French film festival, *Monsieur Hire*. I asked you to come with me for a walk, just to Delta Park or Emmarentia, round the lakes. I was sitting in my flat battling with that caged-in feeling I sometimes used to get on weekends in Yeoville, when I didn't have plans. You said you couldn't, you were busy. That's how I knew you'd be there.

After you two strolled down the passage to the parking garage, I took my time, finished my tea, waited so you'd be in your car, then I followed you in my bakkie, just a bit of the way down Jan Smuts. It was dark, but my bakkie was pretty distinctive and I just didn't have the balls for it, so to speak. You were going back to her folks' place in Ferndale. I knew the address from looking it up in the phone book. I thought about how the two of you were each staying with your own folks and not together, even though you lived together in Cape Town. Your folks were especially heavy about sex, even though mine had the Christian thing, it was a thin, recently acquired veneer and they were much cooler about things like that. Their philosophy was, "It's your life." They probably didn't get as involved because they had lots of their own hassles, with money and other stuff. My brothers were in the army. The thing with your old lady was that she couldn't deal with the thought of you having sex. I never figured out if it was because she was jealous or because the whole idea of sex was just too much for her. Probably both. Your old man must have slipped it to her at least the once.

Why was I surprised that you got tied up with Diane before things were over between us? I know a lot of the messiness was my fault. I wasn't exactly faithful while you were at varsity in Cape Town. But you'd left me behind. Ag, your fault, my fault, never mind who's fault. We broke up and you found a new chick straight away. Even before we broke up. She was part of the reason we broke up. Just like with you and the chick you were involved with before me too, Susie, was it? Only I didn't think it applied to us in the beginning, because it was true love, what we had. That's what you said, well not in those words, because you've got a way with words that made me want to believe you.

The other weird thing about that time was that if you hadn't been going to see a movie with her, you might well have gone walking with me, or we might have gone to a movie. We used to go for walks, I would cry and beg you to come back to me. You would look uncomfortable, but you wouldn't agree to come back. You wouldn't say anything. You'd wait a bit then change the subject. You would even fetch me from the airport when you moved to Cape Town, and I visited there. We would go for drinks somewhere, the Lord Milner hotel. You knew all these cool places where you could have a drink. The Holiday Inn in Gardens the one time, and there was that short TV star from *Dallas*, Miss Ellie's granddaughter, the one with the long blonde hair. Was her name Charlene or Charmaine? Something like that. Only we didn't know she was coming, just that there was this hectic buzz at the Gardens Holiday Inn, and snacks all put out and it was hard to buy a drink, but you managed. And then we left before she arrived, but it was cool to be there and to feel the excitement and to be too cool to stay and try to rub shoulders with an American TV star. We ate a few of the peanuts and things that were meant to be there for her real fans.

After that you took me back to the place I was staying at in Oranjezicht with an old school friend, Clara, the one who'd married a rich guy, a plastic surgeon. They had gone to bed already, you came into my bedroom and kissed me, and pulled my shirt up, and kissed my breasts. And then you went home to her. And that's why I kept thinking that maybe you'd come back to me someday. Only you haven't and you won't and by now I don't even want you to. And I have moved on, even though it may not seem like it, what with me coming out with all this old shit. But sometimes I get nostalgic, not for you, but for those days, because that was when I was young, and so were you and you knew me, like in those before and after pictures, sometimes it feels like you are the only one who knew the before picture of me, when I was still so serious and innocent. And some-times I wonder if Diane ever questioned what we were doing, and how come she didn't put up a bigger fuss about you seeing me. The times you kissed me or pulled me close to you and hurt my hair a bit when you did it, I didn't beg you to come back to me those times. And you looked a different kind of uncomfortable, especially when you'd leave.

The weirdest time was when we went to see a movie together, all three of us, *Father of the Bride*, what a crap movie, or maybe it was a cult movie. Anyway afterwards we went to this café in Long Street, and I paid, like I was a visiting aunt, who was loaded, only I wasn't. But I did have a credit card that wasn't maxed out. You didn't have a credit card, neither did she. It's funny how in some situations it's the one person who always pays. You always seemed poor to me, so even though I wasn't loaded, I always paid.

The time we went to see the movie, you sat in the middle. Diane was wearing a long black coat and we had to go to the bathroom together, we didn't talk or anything. We just smiled at each other, like we were each trying to sell something the other didn't really want to buy. The movie was about a wedding, can't remember the details, something about rich Americans who have wedding planners. It was weird to be watching this movie about a wedding, I kept thinking of the three of us sitting there in the dark, and I couldn't concentrate properly, even though you could have got that movie even if you weren't concentrating. I should have told you to piss off, or you should have told me to. I have no idea why she didn't put her foot down. But none of us did in those days. We had this whole notion that you could still be friends afterwards. Now I see it isn't really friends, because there are all these things you can't say, can't admit to. You find you're having several layers of conversations at once. It's like telling lies, you have to keep your story straight and remember what you said, what you are supposed to know and not know. It's not relaxing. Which is one of the main reasons it's not like real friends.

I got to wondering if you ever think about me, and if you ever think about how crazy and fucking sad I was when you left me, that I *spied on you*? It wasn't really spying, more like lying in wait, like a lioness might wait in the trees near a place she knows buck will come to. Okay, no you're right, it was a kind of spying. It cured me of spying though, I felt so freaked out and shaky. And it made me see things a bit differently, I saw how it was between you and her. Even though you sweet-talked me, with some of the stuff that you would say and the way you looked at me, after that spying episode, I had my own version of what was going on. I didn't have to rely on your version. So maybe there was something healthy about what I did. Forced myself to confront what was what. It made me sadder than hell and after that I sort of gave up.

Sometimes I remember those days and it's hard to really connect with why I did certain things. It was all so unbelievably intense and over the top. Compared to those days, I am totally chilled now. I thought about that time we went to see that Athol Fugard play at the

111

Market Theatre, the one set in a school. I picked you up in Rivonia; you were staying with your folks for some weird reason, and I drove there on the M1 way too fast, you were shit scared that I would crash on purpose or something. You kept telling me, "Slow down a bit," not wanting to sound as panicky as you felt. The play was pretty good, calmed me down, took me out of myself, so afterwards I drove properly. I kept the ticket stubs in my jacket pocket for months afterwards, to remind me of you and of my own anguish. You know when you have a sore tooth and you keep feeling it with your tongue, like that. I wanted to feel sad, I didn't want to get over you. Nothing worked out for me with other guys for a long time because I would always talk about you – guaranteed not to make the new guy feel important. But in the end, I did get over you. Just like the songs promise.

Co-winner of the SALA Nadine Gordimer
Short story Prize | 2014

Vicious Cycle

RENEILWE MALATJI

I'm not sure why I agreed when Adichie invited me to go for a picnic with him and his Norwegian friend. The combination of Adichie, a Nigerian PhD student at Rhodes and Peter, a professor in the Sociology Department, was usually more than I could bear at a time. It was impossible for those two to snap out of academic mode.

It was a clear November Sunday, with the sun casting its full warm rays on our seats. Adichie and Peter sat in the front of the car while I sat in the back with Peter's two children.

I was quiet for most of the trip. My silence made them uncomfortable because they knew me to be chatty.

"Are you okay?" asked Adichie.

"I'm fine. Don't mind me. I'm just a bit tired," I said.

The truth was that I was intimidated by the two academics' seriousness and lack of humour. I was not in the mood to fight intellectual wars. Nor did I want to be made to feel embarrassed by my ignorance. So I left them to eloquently contest one another from different points of view, even on topics they agreed on.

Since I had come to Rhodes University, I'd learnt to avoid academics as far as possible when I wanted to enjoy myself and unwind. I found it hard to relax while discussing theories and philosophies. I preferred uninhibited, simple conversations and would rather leave the theories for the lecture halls. I had just submitted my final essay and my head was still rattling as if there were tins and nails in it. My brain needed a break. I would have preferred to go and unwind in the township.

I sat there with the five-year-old twins, a girl and a boy. Their father kept on checking them in the rearview mirror and talking to them in Norwegian. They were born in South Africa and had only visited Norway during holidays. Peter bragged to us about how he had single-handedly taught them his home language. Every now and then he paused from his clever talk with Adichie to say something to the children.

I found myself envying the twins. I wished I could go back to my childhood and have a father that was this attentive. Or that I could return to my youth and re-conceive my two boys with a man this caring. I later discovered that Peter was separated from his Xhosa wife and his children were now living with him full time. I wondered about what could have caused the split. If I had a man who cared about children this much, I would never leave him, I thought.

I became lost in my thoughts, as the two men engaged in their intellectual gymnastics. As we drove through the green mountains that separated Grahamstown and the nature reserve, I began to explore the darker tracks of my life. There was a bitter taste in my mouth as my thoughts turned to my father and my children's father.

I recalled how, when he was fifteen, my younger son, Gamza, ran away from home to look for his father. He hitch-hiked to Thoho-yandou town, where Luvhengo, his father, lived. He went straight to the police station where Luvhengo worked and asked for him. He did not even know what his father looked like, as the last time he had seen him was when he was a year old. They told him that he was on leave and would be back in two days' time. My son did not push to find out where his father's home was, as he was afraid that Luvhengo's new wife might not like him. He roamed around the town for two days, sleeping in the graveyard at night. In the meantime, I was looking for him everywhere, and I had filed a missing person's case in Polokwane, where we lived.

On the third day, my son met his father for the first time. Gamza said he was amazed by how much he looked like him. Luvhengo took my son to KFC and bought him a Streetwise Two. They sat and he ate. The boy said he was happy to have met him and had all kinds of hopes for their newfound relationship.

"I want to come and stay with you," my son told his father. "I am tired of my mother's husband calling us luckless and fatherless bastards." Gamza told his father everything, including the fact that my current husband was abusive and not contributing much financially in our home, which belonged to me. Apparently Luvhengo listened attentively, remaining silent for some time. When it was his turn to respond, he said, "Look son, I am happy that you have hunted me down. It is a good thing that we now know each other. You see, life is more complicated than you think. I am a clerk at the police station. I earn very little. I am not as rich as your mother, who is educated."

"Look at you: you are wearing clothes that I cannot afford, even for myself. Nike shoes, a Puma T-shirt ... I know how much those things cost. You probably go to a private school. What I am telling you is that as much as I might want you to live with me, I could never afford to look after you. I have another wife with five children. Our house has two bedrooms, you see."

"Another thing is that my wife fought a lot with your mother years ago. I don't think she will accept you. I am sorry, but you have to go back to your mother. Life with her is much better than what I can offer."

Luvhengo then told Gamza to give him my number, and took out his cellphone from his jacket. I remember how surprised I was to receive a call from him.

"Hello Mapula. It's me, Luvhengo. I am with Gamza here. He said he hitchhiked—"

"What? Where?" I interrupted him. He then ran out of airtime and I had to call him back.

"You must come and fetch him. I told him you are a good mother," said Luvhengo. I was so annoyed with him for rejecting my son like that. But I wasn't shocked, because he had never cared enough to contribute a cent towards bringing up the two boys. I hadn't even bothered to take him to the maintenance court.

I told Gamza to meet me at the Caltex garage. I warned him not to bring his father along as I might kill him. He couldn't even make a plan to get his son back home. In the car Gamza was mute. I did not say anything either. I could see the hurt in his black eyes. I left him alone with his thoughts and focused on my own anger.

It was overcast that day. Large silver clouds drifted slowly across the sky, now and then obscuring the sun. I hated cloudy days. It was a grey-sky day when Luvhengo left me with two kids for a younger woman. And it was hazy the day my recent husband first hit me and called my sons bastards.

A few days later, when the anger had subsided, I appreciated the fact that at least Luvhengo had been upfront with my son. I recalled the incident of Mumsy's son, who also went looking for his father. The boy found out that his father was in fact a well-to-do someone – or rather he gave the boy that impression. He promised the boy all sorts of things – a PlayStation, a bicycle, new clothes, and to take him out of government school so that he could go to a private school like his step-brother.

Mumsy warned her son not to get too excited as his father was the most unreliable person she had ever known. But the boy chose to believe him. They had set a date on which they were going to meet to buy all these things. The man did not pitch, nor bother to postpone. From that day on he avoided the boy's calls. When Mumsy's son used a public phone, he dropped the phone as soon as he heard the young boy's voice. One late afternoon on a Tuesday, Mumsy came home from work, tired. She opened the garage door to park her car, only to find her worst nightmare. Her son was hanging from the garage ceiling.

I talked to my son and told him that it was not the end of the world. I assured him that his father's rejection did not define who he was, and that it wasn't his fault. It would only affect him if he allowed it to. I said that there were many great men who had grown up with absent fathers. I told him the story of Walter Sisulu. Sisulu's father, a white man who employed his mother as a domestic worker, died denying that he was Walter's father. And look at how successful he became. He was now a world-known icon who had fought for South African democracy.

Gamza's face lit up, and he said, "Mom, don't worry. I am fine. I understand."

I was relieved. "Now don't go and do anything stupid – like committing suicide without discussing it with me first," I said, and he laughed.

A month after that incident, my new husband asked me for money to install a music system in the car that I had bought for him. When I refused, he shouted at me, calling me a selfish bitch. He told me that he had done me a favour by marrying me, with my two bastards, as no other man would have done. He was shouting so loudly that I was sure my sons could hear him. I decided to shut myself in my office and catch up on some work, to distract myself from my angry thoughts.

That day my two sons, fifteen and seventeen years old, decided it was time to discipline my husband. They knew he hated loud music and played it anyway. When he came downstairs, he screamed at them as usual, telling them that they should go and live with their father because they were disturbing his peace. Normally my sons would have kept quiet and lowered the volume.

"If you want your peace, why don't you go and buy yourself a house? Like a normal man. This is our home. You found us staying here. You must adapt to our ways or go to wherever you came here from."

"If it was up to us, you would not be living in this house. We are just putting up with you because we have no choice,' said my older son, Rudzani.

"What?" my husband responded.

"We are sick and tired of your verbal abuse. Go and feel sorry for yourself in your own house and abuse your own children, if you have any," the boy added.

"Just who do you think you're talking to?" my husband raged. "How dare you! You don't know me. I will ..." He tried to punch Rudzani, but Gamza came from behind and hit him with his cricket bat. The boys were stronger than my husband had imagined. At that moment they attacked him jointly, overpowering him. Side tables and vases were knocked over as he stumbled out of the room and headed upstairs. He burst into my office, where I had been listening to the altercation, hoping to avoid having to get involved.

"I can't live with those savages anymore. I am going. You can call me when they are no longer there. Maybe I will still be available," he said.

"What do you want me to do? Kill them? They are my children. You are the one who has turned them into monsters. They learnt violence from you," I said.

"Then you must sleep with them. I am going," he said.

"Where will you go?" I asked.

"Don't ask me questions," he said.

"Okay," I said quietly.

I was tired of him treating me like I should be grateful to have him. I was drained by his abuse, his irresponsibility and sense of entitlement. Fortunately we were married out of community of property. The wisest decision I ever took with regard to him. I'd insisted on it despite his efforts at dissuasion, as I had a lot more to lose.

After leaving, he did not call and nor did I. I realised how much happier my sons were without him in the house. I felt bad for having put them through a fatherless childhood and then imposing a useless husband on them. I decided it was time for a new start: a divorce and a change of career. That is how I ended up back at Rhodes University. I enrolled my sons at St Andrew's College in Grahamstown. It was one of the best schools in the country. The small university town was a different world from Limpopo, where people were defined by their marital status.

"A penny for your thoughts," said Adichie from the front seat.

"Oh, I was just daydreaming," I said.

The reserve was beautiful. At the gate there was a viewpoint from which one could see the river circling the mountains like a necklace. I now understood why it was called Water's Meeting.

The reflection of the trees made the river water green. I could have stood there for hours, taking it all in. We drove down a rocky gravel road to the river. There was a picnic spot with wooden tables and benches and a braai area. Peter helped the twins change into their swimming costumes. He then gave them their padkos-biscuits, juice and apples. In my world, men who did what he did for his children were as scarce as Indian policemen in Polokwane.

The river water was clear. Peter jumped in and floated with the girl on his back, holding the boy in front. It was a perfect picture of fatherhood. I watched them while sitting on the concrete bridge-like structure that crossed the river, with my feet in the water. I couldn't believe I was jealous of five-year-olds. I tried to entertain myself by counting tadpoles in the water. I stirred them with a stick and was amused when they swam in different directions. Adichie sat within talking distance of me, reading the *City Press* newspaper.

"Is he sure this water is safe? Are we sure they don't have crocodiles here?" said Adichie, and I laughed.

"They would have written a warning if there were," I said.

Adichie was a short, middle-aged man who always over-empha-sised what he said, as if you wouldn't believe him otherwise. Everyone acquainted with Adichie knew that he couldn't have a conversation with any South African without comparing their country to Nigeria. With him, it was always, "In Nigeria we don't do this" or, "We do things like that." He would always mention that he had been an associate professor at a Nigerian university but had done his other PhD in the USA.

When I first met him, I thought he was strange. But by now I had grown used to him, and had stopped judging him. My phone rang and it was my mother. Since I left Limpopo, we'd speak on the phone a few times every week. I stood up and walked across the bridge, trying to find better reception. Adichie went back to his paper.

"It must be a boyfriend you were talking to for so long," said Adichie.

I laughed. "No, it was my mom. Updating me on the latest from back home," I told him.

"You know I've noticed that you black South Africans always talk about your mothers. But never your fathers. Why is that?" he said.

I felt like he was reading my mind. I tried to turn the conversation back to him, teasing. "Adichie, I think the second PhD is driving you mad. Too much reading is not good for you," I said.

I knew what was coming. This was a sensitive topic for me. I feared conversations about fathers the way other people feared dentists. I knew that men lacked the sensitivity to speak the truth with care. I had also become aware that most of those who grew up with fathers were painfully unsympathetic and insensitive to those who hadn't. That is because they didn't know how it felt. A man who was pursuing me once said on our first date that most people who were not raised by their fathers were abnormal. "They always have some kind of issues," he said. I didn't dispute his theory.

I was not ready to venture into this topic with Adichie. But he persisted.

"You know what I am talking about: most men here abandon their children. In Nigeria, that never happens at all."

"Really?" I said.

"Yes. It is an embarrassing situation. Do you know a bird does better than most South African black men when it comes to looking after its youth? And it doesn't even have a job," he said. I forced a laugh and saw him examining my face.

"You know this thing started when people were migrant workers, coming home twice a year. Those boys who grew up under those conditions were never taught by anyone how to be a father. Father-hood is a learnt behaviour," said Adichie.

He was right. I could think of very little evidence of enchanting father-and-child relationships among black families in South Africa.

After a long walk in the forest, we were finally back in the car and on our way home. Adichie and I did not enjoy the walk as much as Peter and his twins, who loved hiking. Adichie kept on hinting that it might not be safe, as lions and leopards could have crossed from the local game farms to look for food.

Sitting back, I left the two men to resume their conversation. This time Adichie was defending Africa. "Africa is the butt of every international joke. You Europeans should leave us to live our own lives the way we know best," said Adichie.

"You say Africa this, Africa that, and yet there would never have been an Africa if we hadn't come and discovered it and even named it for you," said Peter. I was amused by the way Adichie was not offended by this statement.

As the two men continued throwing word missiles at each other, my thoughts returned to the men in my life. I recalled the day, five years back, when I met my dad for the first time.

I had accepted that he was not part of our life and I did not think much about him. It is difficult to miss a stranger. I felt some sense of loss over not having a biological father, but not over him. My step-father had raised us well. But for my brother, this was not enough. He was obsessed with meeting his real father.

That day, I drove my mother and brother to a place called Mtititi, on a mission to find our father. The village was in the middle of a dense forest, near the Kruger National Park. We drove through the heat on the rough gravel road, finally arriving in the late afternoon.

The first building we came across in Mtititi was a small, flat-roofed school, beyond which was a cluster of rondawels. We soon got lost: it had been many years since my mother had left the village. The women we stopped to ask for directions took a quarter of an hour greeting us. They laid out their whole lineage to us, as if it were the most important thing in the world, and they were eager to share tidbits of village gossip.

The mud huts gave the rural settlement an ashen look. The August winds were wild and dust from the dry earth spread everywhere. Everyone's face was made up with a brown mascara of dust.

"Your father did me a favour by leaving me. Imagine! I would still be stuck in this place, rotting like an over-ripe tomato," said my mother. "I would have never studied to become a teacher. You, Tshepo, would be minding some chief's cattle for no salary. Look at this place, there is nothing. Where would one get a job here? It's far from every-thing."

My father, who had worked in Johannesburg most of his life, was now back in his home village. Shortly after I was born he had abandoned my mother and us and gone back to Johannesburg. After several years, when he did not return, my mother packed her belong-ings (including us) and left.

Finally we arrived at my father's home. The yard was big, like most rural yards, and they had planted corn in the back. I saw three goats tied with a long rope to some trees towards the left of the plot.

A small, windowless thatched hut stood in the centre of the yard. A dirty cloth served as a door. A short adult would have to bend to enter the hut. Then there was a small square house built recklessly from grey block bricks. Its windows had no glass; instead, a sheet of corrugated iron covered the window spaces.

A thin woman wearing an oversized brown dress with a matching pinafore met us at the small gate. "It must be the wife," whispered my mother as she approached and directed us into the grey house.

Walking close to her, I caught the scent of baked earth coming from her emaciated body.

Inside, the air was stifling. Harsh coughing sounds could be heard from another room. There was a wooden bench and a small table in the corner, around which were a few white garden chairs. Plastic crates pushed beneath the table served as cabinets. The linoleum-tiled floor was sticky with grime and dust. My mother looked at me and shook her head. "Please, can we rather sit outside in the shade? The heat in this house is making my blood pressure rise," she said.

After a while, a man came outside and walked slowly towards us. He wore a pair of old, torn jeans and a shirt that was frayed at its hems. His complexion was dark, but the undersides of his arms were lighter in tone. He had an odd way of walking, as if he were being pushed from behind by a gust of wind. The sun was now concealed by patches of dark cloud. It seemed like it was going to rain.

So this is my father, I thought. I was not impressed. The whole thing did not feel real. I felt like I was in a movie. It was obvious that my brother felt differently. He stood up from the bench and remained standing until the older man sat down next to him. My brother's eyes were filled with tears. I wondered if these were tears of joy or something else. His life was in chaos. He had been fired from his job at Ackermans because of drunkenness. I was now supporting him and his family financially.

I felt nothing for my father. I decided the whole venture was a complete waste of time. I was only interested in how much the man looked like my brother.

"Mokope, how are you?" the man said to my mother. His smile exposed his missing front teeth. His eyes were dull and the lids heavy, so that he looked as if he were about to fall asleep.

"I am fine, I have brought your children," she said. I could not understand why she did not seem to be angry with him. Maybe it was because she had moved on, got married and found happiness with my step-father.

He stood up and shook our hands. His hand was rough against my palm. I hated myself for being so unmoved, but I just could not help it. From his wrecked appearance, it looked like he had paid for even his future sins, I thought.

"You are all grown up. The last time I saw you were just babies," the man said.

We just looked at him and kept quiet. I wanted to ask him why he had not come to see us in all those years. But it was pointless, I thought. It wouldn't change anything. My eyes moved to the goats that were grazing. I could not understand why they had to be tied to the trees. I wondered how I would have felt if I was one of them. Maybe I am a goat, I thought. I am also tied to men who couldn't care less about me.

"They are both working now," my mother was answering for us. "Mapula works for the government. They now have their own children." My mother was one of those people that never mentioned her children's failures to anyone. She did not say a word about my brother's dismissal from work. She viewed us as an extension of herself, and our misfortunes became hers too. When I went through a divorce, it was as if it were my mother's marriage that was ending, not mine. Sometimes I felt like her pain was worse than mine.

"Mhh! A government job! That is good. My girl, maybe you can buy your old daddy a small van so that I can sell tomatoes in the village. I have a licence. I was a truck driver in Joburg."

Something snapped in me and I started hustling them to leave.

"I have work to do in the office," I said. I regretted the whole exercise. It had been futile. I was even more irritated when my brother hugged him.

The memories of my father still chafed as the car drove into Grahamstown. Peter dropped Adichie and me at the Spur. Adichie had offered to buy me supper.

"You are very quiet," Adichie said while we were waiting for our steaks.

"I was just thinking about what you said," I told him.

"We can't blame these men for not being involved with their children," said Adichie.

"Why?"

"Because, like I said earlier, love is a learnt thing. It is through the love of a father that you learn how to be a father. Their fathers were never there – they were working in Johannesburg in the mines. So this thing has become a vicious cycle," he said.

"Well someone should break it. Things can't continue like this. Men don't seem to feel the slightest guilt about the children they've fathered and then abandoned. It is the most normal and acceptable thing in black communities. I respect the white brothers for seeing things differently," I said.

"I don't know. You are the writer. Maybe you can create awareness and make people start debating solutions. But if you South Africans don't do anything you will end up with a very angry youth. The signs are already there. Take for instance this ANC Youth League president Julius Malema. I don't think he was raised with a father present."

I was chewing my steak when he said that. It tasted like a facecloth. I struggled to swallow, but eventually it went down. I looked at Adichie and faked a smile again.

"You know what? I am going to get a doggy bag. I will eat this later. Thank you so much," I said.

I felt my anger subsiding. An urge to forgive my father suddenly came over me, and for the first time that I could remember, I was able to feel pity for him. Leaving the Spur that evening, I felt hopeful that one day all my hatred would fade, maybe even vanish like clouds when the sun comes out.

Co-winner of the SALA Nadine Gordimer
Short story Prize | 2014

Prayers

MAKHOSAZANA XABA

My name is Refiloe. I am thirteen years old. My sister Lesedi is four. My parents passed away last year. Papa went first, three months before Mme.

It all began in February last year, when Papa came back from the mines in Johannesburg. An ambulance dropped him right in front of our home, too ill to walk and talk. The driver of the ambulance spoke to Mme for a long time as the neybars helped carry Papa into the house. He told Mme how difficult it was to find our village because it is tucked away between two hills, and he is not used to driving in areas where there are no road signs. And the roads are very bad. What he didn't know is that the roads were once horrific. At least now they are wider and that makes it easier for cars, now two cars can stand alongside each other. This means that the road does not get used up too quickly, and on rainy days mud does not accumulate too fast, making them impassible.

I remember that day when a man came from the government offices to talk to all the elders in the village about the plans to improve the roads and install a water pump for our village that we could all use instead of going all the way to the river. Mme was delighted, so was I. We had a water tank that my father bought years ago, when I was seven. But in winter when there are no rains, we use up all the water and have to go to the river. I hate walking to the river in winter, it gets dark very early and the shadows of the hill make it so much colder than it really is. The river is right next to the foot of the hill, where it really freezes.

As I was saying, the ambulance driver complained to Mme. He said he had to stop many times asking people where to find Moosa's General Dealers, our main store. Apparently that was all my father could tell him because he was very ill and could not talk much. Although I was very sad to see Papa like that, I was relieved that he had come back home. As Mme kept telling us, "It's much better to die with your family, with love around you and prayers for your future life." Everyone thought Papa would pass away very soon after he arrived home. Many people now say Mme's love kept him alive.

Granny-next-door (her village nickname is very rude, Mme said we could just call her Granny-next-door) kept telling Mme that the reason Papa was staying alive for so long even when he was in such pain was because our ancestors were still paving the way for him in their land. Apparently there is a special way to be when one arrives in that land. She also said that although we could neither see nor hear Papa talk to them, she was sure it was happening because the ancestors speak in a language we cannot understand. I asked Mistress Maluleke about ancestors. She just said I must wait till I am older: "Understanding ancestors comes with age and maturity, child." Most old people in my village talk about ancestors a lot, but they don't want us present when they have these conversations.

Now back to Papa. He passed away six months after the ambulance dropped him off. Many neybars I heard talk to Mme said she was very brave to nurse him until his last day when the hospital could have taken care of him very well. But Mme had one belief; if the hospitals in Johannesburg had sent him home, our hospital in town couldn't do anything better. It's the longest time I remember spending with Papa. As a mining man he only came home for the Christmas and Easter holidays. There were years when he did not come during the Easter holidays because he had no money. One of those years was the year my sister was born. Mme said he had to buy extra food and so many baby clothes that he simply could not afford money to come home. Mme also said this was the life of all mining men in our village. They hardly ever saw their families because there is very little money paid to them. It takes a long time to dig gold, diamonds and coal from the stomach of the earth. Sometimes they could dig for months without finding even the smallest piece. The bosses paid the miners only when they dig enough gold and diamonds. Mme always prayed that Papa could find a job in a gold or diamond mine because the mining men were better paid in those mines. Papa was in a coal mine that was notorious for paying very little because South Africa did not sell coal to other countries.

I hope I have not bored you with this long beginning, full of recent history. Mistress Maluleke said I must "paint pictures" when I tell this story. Our lives depend on it.

So here is what I should have started with. My school is called Lesedi Primary School, LPS for short. It's one of the schools built by the former President Mandela. It's big and beautiful. It is so beautiful it looks lost among the village houses. In this village, many children born that year were named Lesedi, just like my sister. I will not say much about our school. Mistress Maluleke will be able to tell you much more about it than I can. She will also tell you about how well I perform in class. She can give you all my reports if you need them. I am now in Grade Seven, my last year in primary school.

Before I go any further I want to apologise for calling you "you", as I tell our story. In our culture it's rude to call an adult "you", but Mistress Maluleke said I must call you like that as she thinks it's acceptable in your culture. Also, she does not know your name. She said she would write covering letters once she has found out all your names and made copies of this, our story, to send to as many businessmen as possible. That is the only chance we have of getting money to make our prayers and dreams come true. Everyone at LPS says it was Mistress Maluleke who wrote many letters to Papa Mandela asking him to build a school for us. She even travelled to Johannesburg to talk to Papa Mandela. When I asked her if that was true, she just smiled and said, "I just did my bit, child". The children want her to become the principal.

Now let me tell you about what Lesedi and I do each day. I wake up at 5am. I cook soft porridge for the two of us on the primus stove. I always make enough for breakfast and lunch if we have enough mieliemeal. While the porridge is cooking I go to clean our toilet. We still use pit toilets in our village, but ours is one of those nicer ones. Papa built a wooden seat so that we don't have to squat. It even has a lid that Papa made with his own hands many a Christmas holiday ago. Mme trained me to clean the toilet in the morning before it becomes too hot. The problem with too much heat is the flies and the smell. I don't mind the flies because I am used to them. It's the smell I can't stand. Now that we don't use wood for cooking, we don't have ash to throw down the toilet. The ash acts as air-freshener and it's just one of those things you cannot ask the neybars for because they use all theirs. It takes a lot of ash to take the smell away. Unlike salt that you only need to use a little at a time. The complicating thing is that I also cannot use a lot of soap. You see, soap also helps to deal with the smell, but even soap is becoming scarce. I save it.

Here is one area where Mistress Maluleke and I disagree. I will tell you about the others later. She said I must feel free to tell you my opinions as part of this story. She seems to think that I am not "as frugal as your mother was". I swear to you, my very name is frugal. She keeps telling me to live "parsimoniously". I always tell her, "Mistress, our very existence is parsimony."

Once the porridge is done, I wake Lesedi up and pray. Each night I pray that she doesn't pee in her bed. As I wake her up I also pray because there are days when she does it just before I wake her up. That is when I find that it's still hot and smells fresh. She sleeps on her own grass mat on the floor next to my bed. I make her sleep naked so that I have just one thing to wash because soap is such a problem. But I know that I cannot do that once winter comes. When Mme passed away, Lesedi went back to infancy.

This is where my first plea to you comes in. I have heard that there are tablets that Lesedi can take to help her stop urinating in her sleep. I am told they are very expensive. Your money will go a long way to help us with this. I would really like her to stop as it is affecting her. She starts talking to me rudely, you know, just plain disrespectful. I slap her when she speaks to me like that. Something happens to me, I know I should be patient with her.

If Lesedi's bed is wet, she takes forever to awaken. She turns and turns in her bed until I shout her name or slap her a little on the back. Once she is fully awake, I wash her face and private parts with very little water in a plastic bowl. I use the same water to wash her sheet.

I don't mind it so much when she wets herself over the weekend because that's when I do our washing. Mme said one should never ever leave soiled bed sheets unwashed: "It's unhygienic". She liked to use that word. Mme was a cleaner at the village clinic, so she knew all about it. She used to wash Papa's sheets and pyjamas every morning and as soon as he had messed on himself during the day. Luckily for me, Lesedi does not do the other thing in her sleep. Granny-next-door said I must not use napkins on Lesedi because that would be as good as giving her permission to wet herself. I think she has a good point. What do you think?

The porridge is usually cooked by the time I finish washing the sheet. I dish up the porridge, then put it aside to cool down. Once I finish the washing I wash my face and private parts quickly, just two hands full of water and a dash of soap. The problem comes with that time of the month. Blood is hard to wash out. It needs a lot of water and soap. Fortunately for me, I don't have to buy those expensive sanitary pads. I use the napkins that Mme used for Papa when he could not help himself. They were made from Lesedi's napkins that Mme sewed together to fit Papa. I cut them all up into small pieces and they work out fine. But they are not easy on the soap.

When we have eaten and dressed, I put Lesedi in our wheelbarrow and we go to school. We usually leave our house any time after 7am and definitely before 7.30am. Our school starts at 8.30am because many children come from very far away. It takes me just under an hour to reach school. I always leave Lesedi at Tsidi's home, which is just four homes away from school. I started doing this when Mme was still around because she and Tsidi's mother were very good friends. When Tsidi's mother also passed away, we agreed I could just continue doing this because Lesedi and Tsidi's baby sister have always been good friends.

Now allow me to take some time to tell you a side story about the wheelbarrow. Mme bought it from a farmer on the other side of the hill so that she could take Papa to the clinic once a week, as she did not have money for a taxi. Her salary went down to nothing after Papa came home because she started working only part-time at the clinic so she could be home to nurse Papa. She was attacked, verbally I mean, by many women for doing this. They called her a witch. They said it was undignified to put a man in a wheelbarrow, that she should be ashamed. Some said it would bring bad luck to our family.

This is one thing that Mme and Granny-next-door agreed on. She told Mme to just do what she thought was right and ignore the "stupid village women". And now I put Lesedi in the wheelbarrow, it makes my life so much easier. Granny-next-door gave me a big plastic that I put over Lesedi on rainy days. It's big enough to cover her completely. I use the same plastic between the grass mat and the sheet for Lesedi. That way I don't have to wash the grass mat. I used the wheelbarrow to take Lesedi to the clinic once when she was ill. On days when I don't feel like carrying the bucket of water on my head, I also use it. When I visited my uncle who lives two villages away, I used it. I will tell you about him later.

This brings me to my second prayer and my second disagreement with Mistress Maluleke. I pray every evening that a businessman will build a home for children, orphans who do not go to school and those who do not have homes. With that I would not have to feel bad about leaving Lesedi at Tsidi's home every day. Tsidi has two baby sisters. One is Lesedi's age and the other is only two. The younger one falls ill very often, and Tsidi has to miss school. Tsidi's father is a mining man just like Papa was, and he has never come home since their mother passed away. Fortunately for Tsidi he sends money every month.

Mistress Maluleke says, "There is money out there to give to AIDS orphans, the only question is how to access it." And I disagree. I think if there's money for AIDS orphans, there is money for orphans of any kind. That boy Mbuso is also looking after three siblings. Their parents were killed in a car accident when they went to a wedding in

Johannesburg. Mbuso goes to high school in the next village and works after school and on weekends at Moosa's General Dealers. His brother and sisters are always at home alone until the store closes at seven. I whispered in his ears that Mistress Maluleke is making me write to you, that he should write as well. I mean, he is really a nice boy. Sometimes when I don't have enough money for soap, paraffin, candles and mieliemeal, he gives me some from his home. He once gave me margarine, such a luxury! Mr Moosa pays him in kind some times when he runs out of things for the house. So really I don't buy this "AIDS orphans" story that Mistress Maluleke calls "a fenomenon of our times".

Granny-next-door agrees with me on this. She was born in 1918 in the year when thousands of people died of influenza. She was lucky to have survived, with both her parents. She says she remembers that her own mother used to talk about how unfair it was that the whole community was more concerned about "influenza orphans" than other kinds of orphans. She says what is happening now with AIDS is just history repeating itself. And that history has to repeat itself because human beings take long to learn lessons about life. Granny-next-door speaks about a lot of things this way. I like listening to her though sometimes I think she speaks in confusing ways. Whenever I really miss Mme, I go to her to cry. Her sight is half gone so I don't mind crying in front of her. She tells me that nature has a way of dealing with things. She says this AIDS is here to "level things out", sometimes she calls it "creating a balance". She says all of us will become better adults for having experienced parenting as children.

When I arrive at Tsidi's, she finishes whatever she is doing and we walk to school together. It saddens me that she has to miss so many days when her baby sister is ill because she does not have brightness genes. Granny-next-door says the reason I do so well in school is because intelligence runs through my blood, my genes. After school I sit with Tsidi so we can do homework together before we go to face our sisters. It takes me a long time to get her to understand some of the things I help her with, particularly mathematics, science and English. Unfortunately our teachers are not as patient with those of us who are not so bright.

This is part of the reason I want to be the Minister of Education in my province one day. I really enjoy teaching less smart children at LPS. Do you know that I have already taught Lesedi to count up to twenty, yet she is just four? Granny-next-door says it's the intelligence genes doing that, not me. I hate it when she takes away my credit. It's a pity that when I am the Minister, she will be long gone. There are many things I will correct when I become the Minister. Everyone, including Granny-next-door in her grave, will know that I did it.

Sorry, I went off a bit there. I have been writing this story for three days now. Tsidi wrote hers in one day, just one page, and gave it to Mistress Maluleke. I write a few pages before I start my homework. I then take it to the staffroom for safe-keeping in Mistress Maluleke's desk. She said I could write as long or as short a story as I liked, just as long as it is full of "pictures" for you to really understand our lives. Knowing Mistress Maluleke, I imagine that many children in other grades who also lost parents to this disease are also writing their stories. I have to go now. Till tomorrow, then.

"Mediocrity is the biggest problem black people impose upon themselves in this new South Africa. Women are better at it than men."

You guessed right, that's Mistress Maluleke speaking. She likes saying that. She said it again today in class during our Life Orientation period. When she says that, anger shines through her eyes and she punches the table and desks with her fists. But when she says that, I feel inspiration. I tell you this because she said I must explain in my story what keeps me going. I've never told her this, but each time I hear her say that, I begin to think positively. I don't want to be mediocre, ever.

When Papa passed away Mme went back to work at the clinic full-time. But a month later she was also ill. The head nurse at the clinic, Matron Sithole, said she would find a bed for Mme at the hospital because she knew the senior nurses there. She liked Mme very much. She said she was "a hard-working woman of little education". Mme first resisted going to hospital. Matron Sithole insisted. Granny-next-door persuaded Mme to accept Matron's offer by telling her that if her health worsened and I had to nurse her, I would have to miss school. That changed Mme's mind. So our routine changed. Every Friday afternoon, Matron sent Lesedi and I to visit Mme at the hospital. We went in the clinic ambulance. We would come back in the same ambulance on Saturday morning.

At the hospital they let us sleep there, Lesedi next to Mme and me with the "nursing mothers". These are women whose children are too small, so they are not allowed to go home until the children are big enough to survive outside of the, I think they call them intubators. How can I describe them to you? They are like little tents, made of glass so that each mother can watch her child growing. They have holes for the nurses and doctors put their hands through to touch the babies. Nurses and doctors never let me go near the intubators. I only saw them through the window.

Granny-next-door and some nurses said Mme was killed by exhaustion and a sore heart because really she was never as ill as Papa was. She could still walk to the toilet by herself, although she looked weak, and she played hand-touching games with Lesedi and told us stories right until the last day. Granny-next-door was sad that she never had a chance in those six weeks to visit Mme at the hospital.

Back to our daily routine, Tsidi doesn't like it very much when I help her with schoolwork during the homework period at school. On those days when I do not manage to persuade her to do homework at school, it's the first thing we do when we arrive at her home. When that is done we play with the children a bit, then I take Lesedi's wheelbarrow and we go home.

The first thing I do when we arrive home is work in the garden. Granny-next-door has a vegetable garden that she makes me work in for pay. I make R2.50 a week. Plus she says I can pick whatever I like. Her gardener is always picking enough to feed his family. For supper I cook stiff pap. In good times I mix it with something or put it on the side. Lesedi's favourite is potatoes mixed with pap. I prefer spinach. That day when Mbuso gave me margarine I added it, and as we say in our part of the world, "you couldn't give it to the blind".

Granny-next-door lives with her granddaughter who never did well at school and therefore works in town in white people's kitchens, and comes home every evening. Granny-next-door told me that all her five children still send her money at the end of each month. They send her so much money that she sometimes forgets to go and collect her pension money. She does not have many uses for money. That is why she sometimes gives me brown coins just for making her a cup of her own tea.

I am very anxious about winter coming. We are in the middle of April now. Winter has begun whispering to us. When winter shouts there will be nothing in Granny-next-door's garden for us to have with pap.

I will tell you about our weekend when I write again next week. But to finish off our day, Lesedi and I eat supper together. After supper I teach Lesedi a few things, like today I want her to start counting from twenty backwards. After the lesson I read a bit to her, and then put her in bed. Candles are a big problem with us, on days when I am not as frugal as Mistress Maluleke says I must be, I use so much of the candle! I like to read. I take books from our school library every week. The problem is, there's just not enough time in the day to read. As you will have gathered by now, not one day goes by without me praying before I go to sleep. That's how I end my day.

I hope you had a good weekend. Ours was routine, as you will soon read. After Mme passed away, we used to go to the graveyard every Saturday morning. Lesedi used to talk to Mme for a long time, telling her stories and joking with her. That was one thing I could not stand, hearing her talk like that. It made me so sad I'd start crying. So I stopped going there. We went there this Saturday after a long time, just to clean it up. It was Granny-next-door's idea. I took a grass broom with me and picked up stones and wild flowers on the road. After I finished sweeping, I put the stones and flowers on both graves. Granny-next-door says I should always do this to show respect for my parents and all our ancestors. But she still will not tell me much about ancestors, just like Mistress Maluleke.

The weekend also means cleaning and tidying the house and yard thoroughly. We live in one hut. Our second house that was a proper mud house with two rooms went up in flames soon after Mme went to hospital. Remember I promised to tell you a story about my uncle? This is it. When he heard the news about Mme being in hospital, he came to our house to take all the furniture we had in the second house, even the stove that was in this hut. This hut served as a kitchen and the children's bedroom. The other house had Papa and Mme's bedroom and a living-room. On that day, Granny-next-door and other neybars saw him. He had two other men in the van helping him to move our things. He told them that Mme had given him permission to take everything because we would not need it. Then two weeks later, on a Saturday when we came back from the hospital, we found the second hut in ashes. No one saw anyone but the rumar in the village is that my uncle did it. I never told Mme about it. I made Lesedi swear that she would not tell. When I went to ask him to return some things we really needed, he told me that my family was shameful and he did not want to have anything to do with us. Now, as you know, many people have difficulties accepting this disease, but for me it was hard to discover that it was my family that had such problems. Most village people here have not given us any problems. Even at LPS, children and teachers talk about it as just a disease that we must find a cure for.

As I was saying, I clean the house inside and out. I wash our clothes. That means going to the communal water pump many times. I am usually done by about three in the afternoon. Lesedi often helps here and there. We spend the rest of the afternoon looking for food: fruits, nuts and edible greens that grow in the wild. We also catch edible insects. Almost all the village children do this on Saturday afternoons. Lesedi just loves it. It's not just fun (we play lots of games in the process); it also means that we don't depend on Granny-next-door for vegetables. Mme always said we should live within our means. There was one Saturday when we found so much food we did not need any vegetables from the garden next door. That Saturday I asked Granny-next-door if we could use her paraffin fridge to keep our greens.

On Sunday mornings we go to Sunday school at LPS. This is when I consolidate all my prayers. My biggest prayer of them all is to fulfil Mme's dream. Before Papa passed away, Mme was trying to get his pension money from the mine where he worked. Every Saturday she sent me to Moosa's General Dealers to check if an envelope had come for her. It never came. Mme's problem was that she did not know the name of the mine where Papa worked. She did not know how to follow up. Even Mrs Sithole (the matron at her clinic) said it would be hard to trace the money if Mme did not have the name of the mine. This is where we need your help. Can you please help trace Papa's mine and employer. The information I have on him is the following:

Name: Brian (Boetie) Vukani Lekalakala

Profession: Coal Miner (Digger)

26 Makhosazana Xaba

Name of mine: ? in Johannesburg

Date of starting work: been there since a young man of approximately 25 years

Home village: Bhekilanga Village in Limpopo province

I am still keeping Papa's ID book, as I had to take it with me every Saturday to Moosa's General Dealers when Mme sent me to look for Papa's pension money. I still use it for the same reason, therefore I cannot give it you now. I imagine you will need it for tracing purposes. Just let me know.

If we can get this money, most of our problems will be solved. The money Mme left in her post office account (she did not have a bank account) was only R150. Our post office is a mobile one. It comes to our clinic once a month on the first Friday of the month. With Matron Sithole helping, the post office people allowed me to change the name of the account holder even though I am a minor. She told them I was a "responsible and smart orphaned child-parent". I have been using this money for groceries, and there's now only R25 left. My genes help with my school fees. Mistress Maluleke said I would have no problem getting a bursary for high school and university. But we need the money for our living expenses (mainly food, many candles, paraffin, lots of soap and clothes) and for Lesedi when she starts school. For now she seems to be a bright child, but if we don't get her to stop wetting her bed at night, she might change. I've heard people say bedwetting makes you dull. It affects your head somehow. That would mean she couldn't get bursaries for her education.

I hope that you now have the full picture of our lives. Let me end by emfasising that I am asking that you help us with the three things I mentioned above. If you help us with those, my sister and I will be fully on our own in no time. I therefore appeal to your good heart, your kind spirit and sensibilities, to answer my prayers.

Longlisted for the
Frank O Conner Award | 2015

The Chameleon House

MELISSA DE VILLIERS

Their eyes gave out an eager spirited light that
resembled near-genius, but was youth merely.
– MURIEL SPARK, *THE GIRLS OF SLENDER MEANS*

Ever watched a chameleon backed into a corner? They turn black
with rage. Slowly, of course, but with a strange ferocity, the dark
impulse unfurling over that scaly body like a sombre flag. And all the
while they're keeping tjoepstil, those dot eyes staring in their crazy
turret sockets, one checking ahead, the other behind. You'll stare
too for a while, because there's always a weird kind of glamour in
confrontation, even with a lizard, until it gets bored or you do. You
might think about telling the ragged kid with the stick or whoever's
doing the tormenting to stop prodding the creature, to let it alone,
but most probably you walk on by. There are bigger troubles to deal
with in the world.

That's the way it was with Dena and me. The summer I lived in
London with her I came to see her like that – frightened, stripped of
her camouflage and cornered while the rest of us watched. She and
I, Karen and Tracy, we'd all left South Africa for the first time that
year and even with the glare and roar of a massive new city to nego-
tiate, we were always greedy for something more. So every day we ran,
desperate to keep up, from gigs and parties and underground raves

to the indie boutiques for those grunge threads all the hipsters wore then, always with a portable stereo roaring out Hugh Masekela or the Happy Mondays parked on the end of our beds.

Plus I had other issues, strung out on TJ, my man from back home. I was a liability at work, forgetting change, dropping glasses, yelling at the chefs when my orders went through slow. Nearly got fired for it a couple of times, but I would almost have welcomed that. It was hard to focus on anything much.

I wasn't the only one with a rubbish job. All four of us cadged whatever cash we could – we'd come into the country on holiday visas, no official right to work. Dena scrubbed offices for the White Glove Cleaning Agency in Hammersmith; she'd been there five or six months already by the time we turned up. We joked she must be scrubbing away her white-girl guilt – most people only stuck it out a matter of weeks. Yet she worked longer hours than any of us, turning up her Walkman, squeegeeing and vacuuming, claiming the routine lulled her into a kind of trance. She learned to hold her breath scraping the ammonia crusts off the urinals, she told us, and prising those clotted plaits of slime and hair from the plugs of blocked-up sinks. And she learned to hide how good she'd got at it because if the boss found out, he cut down on your hours to save himself a buck.

We liked it, this city full of restless passersthrough like ourselves. The four of us rented a place together in Collingwood Road, a cramped, litter-strewn street lined with terraced houses whose bulging windows gave them the air of fat men wearing waistcoats buttoned too tight. At night I lay in bed and listened to our Polish neighbour knocking about, watching TV game shows and muttering. Like Karen and Tracy, who shared the sitting room, and Dena, in the box-room at the back, I was always broke, but that was supposed to be part of the whole experience, right? So a couple of days a week I waitressed at Café Koha, while weekends I worked in a pub near Chinatown. I spent the other nights bar-hopping or just getting out of it with whoever happened to be in the house at the time.

No matter how wasted I got, I always seemed to wake when the clock radio would be going off in the Joburg flat, with TJ yawning his way out of bed and feeling sleepily for his jeans, and outside the quivering fingers of the bougainvillea vine stroking the window in the pearly light.

We all knew each other from student days, but Dena and us, we were never that tight. She had had her own crowd back then, and anyway she was reserved; someone with high walls, you know? But now, in her own aloof way, she seemed just as determined to remake herself as the rest of us. Wednesday night was what we called our girls' night out, cocktails and calamari at El Metro in Hammersmith tube station in our new grunge gear and piercings, London-style, while we debated which clubs and drugs we could afford. When we were really skint, we cadged free drinks off a guy Tracy was seeing. He worked the bar at Club Afrique, this basement off the Strand where fixers and go-getters from all over the continent sipped beer and studied the crowd with shining, attentive eyes.

Dena never really let go, though; never got along with the lines of cheap speed and the partying and the pretending to be wild. I kissed her once in some bar late at night, to get rid of a drunk who wouldn't let her alone. I leaned over and kissed her on the mouth, softly but firmly, a long kiss, my hand in her hair, and afterwards she couldn't look me in the eye, although her admirer disappeared without saying another word. She tasted like me – beer and cigarette smoke, plus some odd, sour back note I couldn't quite define. It was rare that she stayed the course, but if she was still around at three in the morning I thought – in the beginning, at least – that it was easy to see what she really was, a nice Afrikaner doedie; sturdy, like most farm girls, in unobjectionable clothes, blonde hair scraped back, laughing politely on cue but always watchful from under her hooded eyes. Efficiently sorting out the taxi home and the house keys as the rest of us stood on the kerb, yelling drunkenly in the street lamps' dirty yellow light.

Still, she stuck around with us because we were cool; at least, we flattered ourselves that we were back then. God knows she needed fun; Dena had been through some tough times. She'd been *involved* – that's what we called it then; part of a network of student activists who'd linked up with the underground movement in exile. No child's play, my china, with thousands of people getting arrested on public violence charges or jailed without trial, and many others beaten, tortured or shot. Eventually, the security police tracked her down in hiding and took her to Port Elizabeth, where she spent just short of four months in the North End jail. She hardly spoke of it, but she told me once that her parents never visited her there. For them, her involvement was a crossing point, a tribal betrayal. Her people were godsdienstige, Dena said; they took the narrow road.

She gave me an ornamental chameleon once, strung with dark blue beads. The kind that street kids make from copper wire. Me and TJ, we had a whole collection of those wire toys in the flat, starfish and bicycles, even a little train, and I told her one time I missed having them around.

For you, she said. So you can start a new hoard. Got it down by PE beachfront, she said. Day they let me out. Couldn't think where to go for a while, so I took the bus and just parked off there by Summerstrand. Watched the moms playing with their kids, the seagulls flocking, ate the best ice cream I'd ever tasted. I had four of them, one after the other! Guy selling them thought I was mal, or high. That country, hey.

TJ and me loved the sea. Liked to camp out on those big, bare Transkei beaches once the rains had come and gone, heading as far north as we could hack it in the 4x4 to where it gets so lush and wild you can stop wearing clothes for days because there's no one around to see. We'd planned to get married up there, throw a big party in Port St Johns, at the Rhodes Hotel. Got the invitations drafted and all. Left my ma to deal with all that stuff; just walked away from it and she never asked what or why. No doubt she had her views.

TJ couldn't get over why I'd done what I did. Listen, it meant nothing. I got out of it one night and pulled an action, I told him. Trying to make him smile, using that old Durban surfer slang he grew up with, but he didn't smile.

He was my man, had been since I was seventeen, and I never meant to do him down. But don't we all do stupid stuff that's no good for you? You do it and afterwards you find there's no going back or feeling relaxed about it or anything like that.

In five years together we'd only spent a month apart, when he went home to Durban after his dad died. The day he got back he spent an age slashing away at the bougainvillea covering the front wall of our flat, trickling its tendrils over the windows and turning the room inside mermaid green. I told him, TJ, leave it, I like the way it falls; it makes our place private, a secret cave we can hide out in. He said no, what we needed was to keep tearing the damn stuff down. He said it's easier than you think to get hooked on living a secret life.

Check this out, half-price deals to Ibiza, Dena said at one of our Wednesday night sessions. We were reading the *Evening Standard*'s travel section out loud, wincing every time the barroom door banged open and a rainy wind blew in. It was early June. The movies paint a picture of these strawberry-filled English summers, with never a hint of how sodden they actually are. We were always fantasising about which foreign beaches we were going to blow our hard-earned bucks on, to try and get warm.

Ja, but a hundred and fifty pounds more gets you to Thailand, where it's thirty degrees right now. This was Tracy, gingerly turning her new nose-stud as she scanned the room. Catch a full moon party on Ko Phangan, dance all night, they say it's like meditation in action. Fully, man. A month there'll sort out all our shit.

I can so picture you there – that place will be perfect for your kind of vibe, my koeks, nodded Dena, with a gracious tilt of the head. We watched as she sipped her beer, waiting until she'd swallowed, replacing her glass right in the middle of the stained beer mat. All three of us had plenty to say, but we waited until Dena said her quiet word first and then jumped in. I thought of the queues that sprouted in shops and outside clubs in this sober northern city, static conga-lines that always seemed so tidy and well-behaved. People here swerved into line like it was a duty; now suddenly we were swerving behind Dena's words in much the same way. It was remarkable, you know, how quickly she took that role away from me, and without even missing a beat.

But that night Karen had something on her mind, and she was all lit up with it.

Listen, Dena. Grant phoned.

Karen's brother. A nice guy, with struggle credentials good enough to net him a reporter's job with the newly beefed-up state broadcaster.

Ja, there's this new documentary coming up, perfect for you. Free tickets home to do an interview and maybe a fee.

Hmm, what – activist stuff? Because, you know, all that's kind of behind me now. Dena pulled a demure face, but she looked pleased.

Of course, said Karen, nodding admiringly. Karen revered Dena like she had the power of healing. It was embarrassing to see – maybe she was hoping some of that I-suffered-with-the-comrades karma would transfer itself to suburban old her. My toes curled for her sometimes, really they did. She pulled her chair closer, her face all stern.

This one's big budget. You know how the government's going public with the old secret police records? So the idea is to film activists from the struggle days checking out their files! All those search-and-destroy dirty tricks, Dena, how the apartheid government harassed the comrades fighting for justice, here's your chance to expose what they did to you! To the world!

Star in a film? asked Tracy, bright-eyed. Nice one, man. Wonder if I've got a police file.

Searched at a roadblock once, weren't you, my sweet? Dena said, quickly. This time, her smile wasn't quite lighting up her face.

Oh my God! That bonehead cop ...

I pressed my lips together to stifle a giggle. We'd only heard this story about a dozen times.

... old as my grandad, patting my arse every which way, siestog man! Must be his worst nightmare to be a policeman with the Rainbow Nation, if he's even still got a job.

You bet. Listen, let's drink to that. And Dena was gone, shouldering through the crowd to buy another round.

By nine thirty the room was filling up, bodies jostling, everyone gulping the drinks down, sweating and smoking, hot and loud. At times like this, with a kind of liquid hilarity rippling through the

room, London seemed the best place in the world. We could be anyone, taking a punt on a new style or image; no one would slap you
down. At first, we had been reluctant to say where we were from – we
were ashamed to be lumped in with all those old crooks and killers
in the apartheid regime. But it wasn't long before we realised that
people didn't seem to care about any of that. In fact, they looked the
other way if you brought it up. Try and explain to a Brit why you
didn't think things had really changed that much back home – that
where you came from, your mom and dad arse-kissed their colleagues
at work but still called them 'kaffirs' round the dinner table, and
eight times out of ten they'd just cough politely and look blank. Most
people seemed quite keen on the idea that the worst was over and
everything was now pretty much on track; it was somehow rather
tedious for them to be called upon to speculate on whether that old
apartheid corpse had simply been shoved in a corner and left to rot.
And that was fine for us too. For us, it was a relief beyond telling
to fit in so easily, like now in this long slow mash-up of music and
talking and lights, everything going trippy as you touched it, smooth
and warm like love.

Tracy's voice cut through a lull. She was laughing at Karen who
was bumping about on all fours, plump calves twinkling in the gloom.
She'd lost an earring, one of a pair of mine. Big, look-at-me earrings,
gorgeous, but fake – just gritty flecks of marcasite.

In the blue-tiled ladies' room, Dena leaned over the basin and
held something up to her face until the mirror danced with shards
of light. In the right light she looked arresting, much more so than
the TV and newspaper images would later suggest, since the camera
always underlined a thick-set cast to her features, ignoring the sinuous nature of her hooded eyes, or the way her mood could transform
her face. I myself never believed in her more than that night when

she found the earring, when I stopped at the door and saw her smile at herself – a private self, wolfishly seductive and strange – and she saw me look, and carried on smiling.

Was that when things between Dena and the rest of us began to go wrong? Because she must have been figuring out her next move by then – the reinvention that was yet to come. Ja, it was about then that something odd took hold of her; something I thought I recognised, but didn't understand. She began to brood, pretending to stay part of the gang without actually being involved. She would giggle automatically at the jokes the rest of us made, keep her hooded eyes down, light another cigarette, gnaw at her nails till they split – anything rather than join in, the way she used to. I remember feeling intrigued at how well she kept it up.

July started out grey and damp, the wettest, they said, since records began. The Saturday the South Africans were scheduled to play at Lords, the rain fell in sheets, shutting us into a pinched and dreary world. All the rooftops echoed with the steady drum of it, and the afternoon grew airless round us like a shell.

Our landlord turned up around six. As usual, he'd brought a bottle of Bombay Sapphire gin, and takeaway pizza in a greasy box. Gulbash Singh was a Glaswegian who talked a lot about the 1980s, his Klondyke years, when he'd been an astrologer to the stars; Princess Di had once paid him a call. Now he spun out a meagre income as Psychic Singh, writing horoscopes for a knitting magazine.

He liked to get drunk with us now and again, usually after he'd had a letter from his ex-girlfriend in Edinburgh – a 'super lady', he called her, who had sun, moon and rising signs all astonishingly compatible with his own. I really love her, he would moan.

Well, why don't you get back together with her, then? I said to him that day. But it wasn't straightforward, it seemed; she was with some-one else now, a woman, and they wanted to have a kid. He'd offered to be a sperm donor and she'd just laughed. I'm like, Damn, what is it with you Brits? Do you always have to look on the bright side?

Didn't take long for Karen to fill him in on how her boet, Grant, had scored a luck with this documentary gig, how Singh must per-suade Dena to quit being modest and take part. She really pushed it. Everyone who hung out with us had to hear the tale, and every time Dena would look away, ride it out with a tight little smile.

Have a drink with us, Dena, my fierce South African queen, said Singh in his most placatory voice.

Cheers, but I'm about to go out. No expression on that pale, pointed face. She was methodically emptying the drying rack, putting pots and cutlery away.

Dena, Dena, Dena, said Singh cheerfully, munching on a pizza slice. You're turning down this chance to shine, but why?

Plenty of others. They'll do just fine without me.

Ha, ha. Tell me. You were a victim, too, yes? You suffered at the hands of those mule-headed Boers, my child. So put the past to rest! Why not?

Done that already, Mr Singh. By coming out here.

Och, Dena. But now that everything is being swept out into the open over there ...

Dena slammed down the pan she was holding and spun around. I'm not needed there any more, she hissed. So leave me the fuck alone, and she ran from the room, banging the door behind her.

It was not her words, exactly, as much as the look on her face that was so startling. Singh stared, his mouth fallen slightly open. For about six long seconds there was no sound but the steady gurgling of the rainwater dripping through an outside drain.

All of a sudden, Singh cleared his throat and pointed to something on the table. Must a man die of thirst in his own house? he said.

His bottle of gin stood on a wicker tray. Karen mixed him another drink and he took a large, thoughtful swig.

Chin, chin, he said, and then: Let me give you a little tip about Dena, my girls.

What?

He took another pull and turned to look at the closed kitchen door. She's not what she seems.

What's that supposed to mean? I said, after a while.

It means, she's not all you think she is, he said, louder this time. Or what Karen's brother thinks she is or anyone else. He had another long swig of the gin. That Scorpio vigour of expression, always so fascinating. She will always be an excitingly unpredictable housemate, my dear friends. My question is, what is going to occur with the emotional intensity of the coming full moon? Do you promise to keep me fully informed?

With a sigh, I set down my glass. I'd been clenching it, and my knuckles had turned white. Of course, I said. We'll watch carefully for the effects of the moon, Gulbash. We'll keep you fully informed.

Like TJ might say, keeping secrets can become a habit. But even those of us who lived with her couldn't say just how or why Dena first got hooked. For sure, it must have started long before the story the newspaper exposés told, that she spent years as a police spy. Ja, she sold her sob story to the papers right after she ducked back home. August rent money still in her back pocket. Singh was terribly upset.

See, once she knew people were going to start combing those police files, they'd soon work out who'd been ratting on who. So she must have seen a bust coming. Running off to London was just one way of putting off the inevitable. One side or the other, they didn't give a damn about her.

Anyway, Dena told the journalists that she started informing at school, final year. Her English teacher had a brother – some big shot cop – who recruited her. She kept going when she got to varsity, where the bucks the white government offered helped pay her fees. She never went to jail. In the end, she got too frightened to stop because her handlers said they'd blow her cover. I was manipulated, she said. I'd give anything to undo what happened, anything. That's what she told them.

Picked her moment, I'll give her that. The country awash with truth and reconciliation and all that. And of course, she found a way to adapt, once the fuss died down. My ma heard she's started up a job placement agency in Johannesburg, finding cleaners for the new black elite. Few things show you've made it like getting someone else in to do the dirty work – that's something all South Africans understand, you know? And that's what Dena was sharp enough to see.

People say, but there must have been clues. Amazing, you didn't guess a thing! And I just smile and say, well, there was a lot going on.

But the clues were there.

I met this guy at a party, right before I left for London. A few weeks later, I went round to his flat in Yeoville and lay with him on his sagging bed, listening and then not listening to the noise of people shouting at the far end of the passage. When I opened my eyes, this is what I saw: his nipples, like apple pips. Our bodies – one white, one brown – joined together. His frowning face as he came.

Three weeks, it took me to build up to that – three weeks of sleepless nights, of burning, of failing nerves; of learning to juggle the burning with the cold-blooded business of getting the damn thing going. Messages, movements, meeting-places: all needed secret negotiation, like spies struggling to protect some tiny, doomed state. Still, I worked it all out, how I'd behave when I came home to TJ and our big sad bed, fingers still wiped with that cheating smell, pumped with my stolen power. Trying all the time not to think about how the other guy had clearly gone through all this before – he knew the ropes.

Afterwards, he saw me back to my car, all the terrors of the Joburg night slinking back into the shadows as we roared down the stairs together, enormous, blazing. We'd had a smoke, we were very high. Couple of times walking through the car park I miscalculated my width, scraping into a bin, and the back of a blue BMW. TJ was waiting for me, arms folded across that faded T-shirt that made his eyes look so blue. The other guy still had his arm around me, one hand touching my breast. I couldn't look as he flinched away. Take it easy, man, he said to TJ. Stammering, hoarse, he was so nervous. TJ said to me, We'll talk about this at home, and I said, Piss off, and got into the car. Left them to it. Stayed at my ma's that night, came back, listened to what TJ had to say and then I went and booked my plane ticket. Stood in the queue at Departures, hips and legs still splotched with bruises from the BMW. Black pearls. A thief's reward.

You know, I was the last person she spoke to in the house before she left.

I remember it was a Sunday lunchtime. I hadn't heard or seen her all day, so I stuck my head around her bedroom door. Didn't knock. I just knew something was going on.

She was still in her dressing gown, her hands prodding and picking at stray threads on the sash. And there was her big green backpack splayed open on the floor, half-full.

It was always so tidy, that room – scraped neat, no books or balled-up tights or messy jars of make-up, just a hot water bottle hooked behind the door, clean blouse on the narrow chair, and on the wall, a souvenir poster from the Globe Theatre in a curly script:

... Love is not love
Which alters when it alteration finds
Or bends with the remover to remove

I had brought some grapes from the kitchen table, the big, purple kind, and I started to eat them, one by one. I made some crack about Dena's poster, about her being an intellectual beacon in this house of degenerates, and she shrugged and said ja, the guy who taught them English at school, for him Shakespeare was a hero. He'd scaredthe hell out of them, too. If anyone needed wrestling into line, Mr Engelbrecht had you stand at the front on an upturned wastepaper bin. When the bell rang, he'd make a big play of kicking it out from under you, like he was scoring a drop goal. You little shits need to learn about *respect*, she said, mimicking his accent, her mouth thin and tight.

Eventually I said it looked as though she was packing up.

Ah, she said, colouring a bit. What, me leave our *little family*?

She went on, But it's worked out well, don't you think? It's been great, us four together.

It was the way she said it, like she was so sure of my answer.

Hope we've provided some entertainment value for you at least, I said. How do we score?

What? she said, after waiting for a while.

How's your mind, Dena, I said. You couldn't care less about our little family really, hey? Because you're so clever. Always one step ahead. Always in control. And now I see you're leaving us; perhaps you thought we wouldn't notice. You don't give a damn about us in the house and there's no shame in you at all.

I don't understand, Dena said. Entertainment value? That's good, that's hilarious. Like I'd choose to hang out with you guys, if I didn't have to? I feel sorry for you.

Sorry for us! I said, laughing, like it was funny.

You're all so try-hard, she goes, with your shiny new nose-studs and your Camden Market clothes. But you're still a bunch of spoilt, over-privileged white bitches underneath. Do you even have a game plan for that – for the way you represent, back home? Because you don't fool anyone over here, you know. The only people you manage to impress are other oddballs, like Singh.

I took a deep breath.

Ja, I said. But the world's a bigger place now, Dena. Nobody gives a fuck where the white South Africans end up or what happens to us. But that's not your problem, Dena, is it? Your problem is your real nature is written all over your face and everybody can see it. I can see it. Think you can ever look anyone back home in the eye again, do you, Dena – you cheat?

I was just going with my hunch, but her face, her pale eyes – I can see the hurt there now, as it struggled with surprise. I remember the effort it took to keep my hands from clenching and my breathing slow. *And here's Belinda Mackenzie with Open Book*, said a radio announcer's voice through the wall.

Dena kept on staring at me, but now she looked afraid. Then she hid her face in her hands and said, almost in a whisper, Don't look at me that way.

And I heard it at last, a familiar, wrenching sound: the same one, choked and raw, that forced its way out of me late at night as I lay guilty and sleepless in the dark, alone.

I walked off and sat in the kitchen, ate some more grapes.

They tasted both bitter and sweet.

Winner of the SALA Nadine Gordimer
Short story Prize | 2016

South Bound

SANDRA HILL

Eleanor is asleep under a jacaranda tree in her daughter's lush Escombe garden. Escombe is no longer part of the Natal Colony, the Natal Colony exists only in the minds of people like Eleanor. Escombe, though still in the same place it's always been, is now part of the Union of South Africa. It is the 20th of January 1923. Eleanor has lived in the Natal Colony for thirty years exactly. She has been married for only one day less.

Gladys's garden is wonderful, but according to Eleanor, not as wonderful as it could be with a little more effort. Gladys's bougainvillea are a riot of cerise, peach and white. Her dipladenias climbing the pillars of the front veranda – a profusion of pink. The creamy day lilies are in full bloom. The lavender is a field of purple and the plumbago hedge, where dragon-like chameleons lurk, is thick with blue ... a cool blue cloud at the bottom of the garden, Gladys thinks. Philemon is hard pressed to keep the monkeys from the guava, mango, paw-paw and avocado trees. Eleanor pays little heed to the real reason Gladys has no time for her lawns, beds, shrubs, hedges and trees. In a quarter of an hour or so, Gladys will lift Eleanor in her stout arms and carry her away from the heat into the cool of the house. It is not the time of year to be outdoors, but Eleanor insists on being in the garden.

'That's the way it's always been,' Gladys confides to her new husband, 'Mother insists and Gladys obeys.'

Eleanor is asleep under a jacaranda tree in her daughter's lush Escombe garden. The barometer has dropped. Eleanor does not notice the thickening of the air, nor how clammy her forehead is. Her chair is covered with blankets and a white sheep fleece. It is the day-bed of a woman whose own padding has melted away, whose bones are dissolving, whose joints have swollen over.

'It won't be long,' whispers Walter to his bride as they lie side by side sweltering in the room next to Eleanor's, the door ajar so Gladys can hear her if she calls out. 'I'm afraid, it won't be for very much longer, my dear.'

Eleanor's book is lying on the grass. It is a very slim volume, the slimmest she owns and the latest addition to her collection, thanks to dear Cora who tracked it down somewhere in London and sent it over. Eleanor cannot hold anything heavier than the slimmest of books, nor can she make the pages turn one by one.

She reads Virginia Woolf's collection of short stories, *Monday or Tuesday*, published by Hogarth Press just two years earlier, in the most random of fashions. A page here, a paragraph there. What does it matter? Would the authoress object? Would she feel slighted if she knew an old (only fifty six mind you) ... would she mind if a woman riddled with arthritis was reading her latest book in so random a fashion that each character seeped into the next? Lily, the woman he might have married, the sad woman in the train, the sleeping Miranda, Castalia, Miss Thingummy. Would she mind that each story was losing its borders?

Eleanor had wanted to read the story 'Kew Gardens', and Gladys had opened the book to the right page, and placed it firmly in her hands. Eleanor reads the description of colours, patterns and plants before her eyes snag on the assertion that one always thinks of the past while lying under a tree in a garden.

Yes, she thinks, yes. That's it. That is what a garden does ... it makes you think of the past, of where you have come from.

Eleanor, thick-fingered, tries to turn the page. Oh bother, now the story is taking place on a train. Try again, Eleanor. Now at a tea party. Try again, fingers. Is this the right page? Is it still 'Kew Gardens', or a different story? Hard to tell. Now there are lovers on the grass, lying under a tree perhaps? He wants to take her hand, but oh, she's offering him her heart!

No, no don't! Never entrust your heart to a man, you foolish girl, idiot woman.

Eleanor, defeated, drops her book on the grass and drifts into a fretful sleep. She groans out loud: foolish girl, idiot woman. The birds, little black-headed orioles, pecking the paw-paw skins the maid arranged on the bird table where Eleanor could see them, hear the groan and fly off. The green mamba napping in the thick foliage of the orange clivias hears it and lifts his head. The monkeys in the mango tree hear it, stop chattering for a moment, and look about, thinking Philemon might be coming. Gladys, her hands mixing a batch of scones for tea, the butter already too soft to turn sifted flour into crumbs, hears it and pauses. Was that Mother calling? Would Daddy have heard? She'd turn the radio down but her hands are sticky with dough, besides it's her favourite programme and in a few minutes, the news. Walter likes her to listen to the news ... it makes dinner more interesting. Besides, Mother had insisted she wasn't to be disturbed till tea time. Gladys goes back to her mixing, back to her programme, hums along with the music. She'll check on the old girl as soon as the scones are in the oven. Pretty warm out there under the jacaranda tree.

Eleanor is asleep under the jacaranda tree in her daughter's lush Escombe garden dreaming about the past. And while she sleeps, she groans a long drawn out groan, as if puzzled, as if vexed. Perhaps she is wondering how it can be that women are still foolish enough to entrust their hearts to men? Perhaps she is thinking of her own choices? Life hasn't turned out the way she'd imagined. What was it that made her leave anyway? Has she ever regretted boarding that south bound ship? And why did she marry that man?

CORA'S THEORY

It was an act of rebellion. That is what it was. And my sister Eleanor paid the price for the rest of her life. I have no doubt it was disappointment that killed her, not the awful climate, not the hardships, not the horrible tropical diseases, those she could weather manfully. But disappointment, that's more insidious: that she couldn't tackle head on in her usual fashion, that she was too stubborn to acknowledge, not to herself and especially not to us. She never said much of course, had to keep face in front of Mama. But over the years her guard would slip, and now and then the odd line or phrase in her monthly letters would let me know how disappointing her new life was, how little it matched her expectations. *At least I have my garden* she would write, or *I'd join the League too if I were home.*

I don't think Gilbert featured much in her decision to go, but his marriage proposal gave her spinning compass a direction different to the one Mama wanted. No, it wasn't about Gilbert – my sister hardly knew him when she boarded the SS Nubian, south bound for Port Natal. They had met one summer when Eleanor, sixteen at the time, had accompanied Lord and Lady What-What to Cowes as under-governess. Gilbert had just returned home from fighting Zulus in Africa. Their romance was brief, just a few weeks and a short exchange of letters, but it left Eleanor heart-broken. She didn't hear from him for almost ten years, and then, quite suddenly he wrote to her and a fresh correspondence sprang up between them. It was wrong of course, for Mama to intercept his letters – but she didn't want to see her daughter hurt again. When Eleanor discovered her perfidy, there was an awful, awful row.

Gilbert, back in Africa by then, must have been perplexed when he didn't get a reply to his latest letter, a proposal of marriage no less, so he wrote to a mutual friend and asked him to find out why Eleanor had stopped writing. I still remember the day he came, that friend of Gilbert's. His name was Mr Clarke, Mr James Clarke.

There was a bite to the wind that made passers-by pull their coats tight about them, their hats low over their ears, as they hurried down the road. We were in the parlour, Eleanor and I. I, busy with some tapestry and she pacing up and down at the window, always restless our Eleanor. Just as I was about to ask her to settle down for pity's sake, she stopped dead still. There was a man walking up the road, glancing at a slip of paper in his hand and then at the cottages. He was not from Stratford, even I could tell that by the cut of his coat. London perhaps? Was it someone Eleanor knew? Was that why she drew behind the curtains, but kept staring out at him? The man stood just outside our house, took off his hat, smoothed down his fair hair and pulled on his sideburns. Eleanor stood immobile, but I jumped up and ran out of the room, calling to Mama that there was a visitor, a strange man at our door. I knew something was going to happen.

That was James Clarke. Eleanor introduced him to Mama as a friend she'd made in Cowes, a brother of Lucy Clarke. Mama was disapproving. She knew Gilbert was also from Cowes and must have suspected a coup. Poor Mr Clarke. He was very polite and kept up pleasantries all through a lengthy tea. When Mama finally put her cup in its saucer, he stood up and said to Eleanor;

'Shall we take a stroll, Miss Lewis?'

'A stroll? But it is bitter outside,' protested Mama.

'Just give me a moment to find my coat and hat,' Eleanor said standing. 'We won't be long Mama. Be sure to keep the fire bright Cora, and do your best to finish up that cloth.'

I clearly wasn't to think of accompanying them. Eleanor pulled on her grey serge coat and winter bonnet, but her gloves would not behave. Here was a finger turned inside out and she had to blow into it and slap it against her thigh, but still it would not cooperate. Mr Clarke took the glove from her and righted it.

I watched them leave from the sitting room window. Eleanor had forgotten to change her boots, by the time they reached Chapel Street, her feet would be sodden. There were not many people outdoors now. Those who were scuttled past them like crabs. But Eleanor and Mr Clarke walked slowly, heads together. I watched them until they turned at the corner.

'You forget I am a person!' Eleanor shouted, barely a minute after Mr Clarke had said good-bye at the door. It was already dark by then and Papa was home, scrubbing his hands at the kitchen sink. Mama was making apple turnovers for afters and I was setting the table. It was still half set next morning.

In one of the very last letters she wrote to me herself, towards the end of 1922, shortly before she had to give up writing altogether (already her handwriting was so poor I could hardly make it out), she said she thought God was probably punishing her for the sin of insurrection, and if so, He must regard it as one of the worst sins a person can commit, for she was suffering terribly.

So perhaps I am right. Perhaps she gave up her home and her family all those years ago just to prove a point. Just to remind us all that she was a person.

MRS TURNER'S THEORY

When Eleanor read to us, it made everything else seem like fiction. A dusk-like softness would fall across the faces before her, a softening and a slowing down, as if every gesture was in slow motion, every sound muted. Only Eleanor's voice existed. The words themselves often escaped me, but the music of them filled my ears. Eleanor's voice was like my mother's hand stroking my head, lulling my mind. Her words would loop and dive around us, tumble at our feet and swim off in the breeze. Then one morning, it was the same morning Captain Maloney announced we'd reach Port Natal within two days, Eleanor stopped reading, very abruptly, just broke off midway through a chapter.

'That is all for now, I'm afraid,' she said, more than a trifle brusquely. 'Mrs Turner, it's time for luncheon is it not?'

She'd caught me by surprise, I was far away, dreaming about summer picnics no doubt, and while I fumbled for the watch I wore pinned to my bosom, she disappeared down the gangway.

The girls were always pestering Eleanor to read to them. Jane Austen's *Pride and Prejudice* was their favourite. They wanted to know what happened to Elizabeth and Mr Darcy – the Dreadful-Mr-Darcy, as they called him. I don't think Miss Lewis, Eleanor that is, cared two jots about the lovers, she was more interested in the magazines borrowed from the Captain, but she always obliged them by reading a chapter or two before going back to her own books and magazines.

Eleanor was a tall, skinny girl with hazel eyes and a mass of dark hair she wore pulled back quite severely, in the way of a governess, and to my mind, quite unattractively. She was a plain girl though her skin was lovely, a real English rose. She wore a cerulean blue skirt, with no hint of a bustle. Her tiny waist was accentuated by a darker sash and widening skirt which flared just above the knee. I remember that outfit exactly: the white shirtwaist blouse with ever so slightly puffed sleeves and the short, matching jacket. It was the only outfit I ever saw Eleanor wearing. The rest of her trousseau went to the bottom of the ocean, as did everyone's luggage, when our ship ran ashore in the River Tagus. Every few days, one of us would stay in our cabin – we were cabin mates Eleanor and I – wrapped in a sheet, while the other would wash her set of clothing and hang it out to dry. It was the only thing we could do under the circumstances.

Eleanor was very bookish, always reading, whatever she could get her hands on, or writing in her little notebook. She seldom joined in the games or play acting, not that she was unfriendly, or melancholy, not at all, she was full of life and thrilled to be aboard, always asking the Captain questions about what she could see from deck. I preferred to keep my eyes on board ship, watching the girls' goings-on from my deck chair. Being somewhat older and already widowed, I took it upon myself to look after them.

'What a lark they are having,' I had commented to Mr Pritchard that morning. I think everyone was excited by Captain Maloney's news, excited and anxious no doubt.

'Indeed.' Mr Pritchard settled himself in a deep wicker chair, pleased I'd invited him to join me. 'It is best they enjoy themselves in the time left to them, my dear,' he said rather familiarly, as one tends to be when meeting under such transient circumstances. Having dined with us each evening since Portugal, he now spoke to me as if he had known me all my life.

'Life can be hard in the colonies, especially for a woman.'

'So I believe.'

'Do you suppose it's the lure of romance that has them south bound?'

'For grooms most of them have never met? I very much doubt it, Mr Pritchard.'

'Ah well, there are some who'd say any husband is better than none.'

'I'm afraid I simply can't agree. Given half a chance there is many a woman who would be better off on her own. But that is not possible in our great Empire, is it now, Mr Pritchard?' I said it lightly, but there was an edge to my voice.

'There, there, Mrs Turner, I didn't mean any offence.'

'All I'm saying is that if these young women had better options they would surely have taken them.' I turned my attention back to the girls who were flocking around Eleanor again. Lord knows if I had had any options I would not have been buttoned into that stuffy black dress, off to live as my brother's perpetual guest in some God-forsaken corner of the world.

Mr Pritchard leaned back in his chair and closed his eyes. The poor fool probably had no idea what to say to women with opinions of their own.

'Eleanor,' the girls beg, 'will you read to us again?'

Eleanor smiles and slips her half-written letter into a magazine and tucks it neatly into her bag. 'What about a different story?' she asks. 'I could tell you a story about an adventurer, a woman adventurer who travels to foreign places just for the sake of ....'

'No, no. We want to know what happens to Elizabeth Bennet , don't we, girls?' It's Ida – ring-leader from the start.

'Really? All right then – where were we? Ah yes, Elizabeth just refused Mr Collins.' Eleanor begins reading. But it wasn't long before she broke off. 'That's all for now, I'm afraid,' she said, more than a trifle brusquely. 'Mrs Turner, it's time for luncheon is it not?'

After lunch I went down to our cabin, knocked and entered. Eleanor was lying face down on her bunk, though she sat up very quickly, embarrassed I'd caught her all to pieces. She certainly looked a sight, her face was blotchy, eyes puffy.

'I told the girls, too much reading must have given you a headache. Do you feel a little better now?' `Her hair, rich dark hair, had come completely undone from its usually sober bun. It made her look younger, hanging loose about her shoulders, more vulnerable. I picked up her hair brush and began brushing it.

'Tell me about this man you are going to marry,' I said after a while. 'When did you meet him?'

'In Cowes, in the summer of '83. Mr Knight, Gilbert, was home on holiday after a stint in the army. I had a day off from my duties.'

'1883. That's a long time ago.'

'Yes, yes it is. Ten years.'

'Have you seen him since, your Gilbert?'

'No.'

'Ah.' I kept on brushing her hair, long strokes from the scalp all the way to the bottom of her spine.

'He went back to Africa just after we met, adventuring. But he has a good job now as a clerk on the railways – a job with prospects.'

'And do you love him?' She was quiet for such a long time, I thought she wasn't going to answer my question. Granted it was very impertinent.

'I don't know, Mrs Turner. I liked him very much when we met, but I was just a child then. So much has happened since. The thing is ...'

'Yes?'

'The thing is I don't know if I am cut out for marriage at all.'

'Some people are cut out for marriage, my dear,' I said, 'and some are not.' There. That is what I said to her, and I still believe it. 'Very few women have the luxury to say no,' I said. 'It's not that we lack courage, but alternatives.'

That is my theory. Eleanor lacked alternatives.

BIG GLADYS'S THEORY

Sometimes I think daughters know least about their mothers, or perhaps being more like them than is comfortable to recognise, we try to hide it, we become forgetful of how very like them we are. At least I am, though I think my father's gentle influence, his placid nature is part of my make up too. It was just that – that placidness of his – that annoyed my mother so. Daddy was artistic, given to day-dreaming, quite happy to sit and do nothing, or so it seemed to Mother, but really he was observing beauty, a leaf, the curve of a branch, the patterns on an emerald spotted dove, the shape-shifting shadows of the frangipani tree, the colours of the gaudy bougain-villeas. Daddy liked to sketch, he had a notebook full of beautiful drawings, but Mother, in a fit of pique, tossed it out. I don't ever remember seeing him sketch again. If he did, he did it in secret.

Eleanor, my mother, was not at all dreamy. She was matter of fact and very organised, a hard worker, tolerated no nonsense – though she loved to kiss and cuddle us, play hide and seek with us in the garden – but only when we were alone, when Daddy wasn't there. She was very clever, and wanted us to be clever too. That was all right for my brother Oliver and much later for little Will, they were natu-rally clever. When I reached my teens, she gave up badgering me to study harder.

'It doesn't matter much I suppose,' she said, 'women have to give up any sort of noetic life when they are married, and I dare say you will marry one day too.'

Mother seemed resentful of Daddy, not just for being placid, but for the way her life had turned out, as if it was his fault. I didn't know what noetic meant at the time, but it was clear Mother felt she had sacrificed a lot for very little. It's true she'd had a very hard life.

Mother arrived in Durban with only the clothes on her back. The very next day, in a little church on the Bluff, she married a man she had last seen ten years prior. Daddy had a house in the new suburb of Berea, and she was obliged to begin her wifely duties immediately. Just imagine, if you can, the shock of it all. Arriving in sub tropical Durban in the height of summer, every day blistering hot and pouring with rain, and Durban a small, scabby little place.

It didn't take very long, a matter of weeks in fact, before Mother was pregnant. My brother Oliver was born before the year was out, and a very sickly child he was, not at all suited to the harsh climate. Mother succumbed to tropical fevers too, and they came down with at least one very nasty bout of malaria each. Between looking after frail little Oliver, coping with her own poor health, and running the house with no mother, no sisters, no family at all to support her, life must have been very tough indeed.

And then I came along, three years later, a robust baby that didn't need (or get) the mollycoddling Oliver got. Mother always loved him most, more than anyone – including Daddy.

War broke out with the Boers - The Second Boer War that is – when I was three years old. Down in Durban we were well away from the worst of it, but then at the beginning of 1900, Daddy, who worked as a clerk for the railways, was sent up to Ladysmith, an important rail town, immediately after it was relieved from a long siege. Mother, Oliver and I followed a little while later and we all moved into a small house. It was painted black and the grounds (you cannot describe them as a garden) were still strewn with shell cases. It was only a temporary home, and as soon as something better came up we moved again, this time close to the railway station and next door to the police station.

Mother started working in the garden immediately. That was always the first thing she did whenever we had to move. One thing I can say for Natal, plants grow even when your back is turned. I remember playing in the bottom of the garden, behind one of the beds mother had planted, plants whose cascading stems were already covered with masses of huge yellow trumpet flowers. While down there I heard horses. It wasn't the sound horses usually made when they came into town, the quick, crisp clip-clop. It was a much sadder sound, and it was the sadness that made me look up. Coming along Lyle Street, was a party of bedraggled horses with even more bedraggled riders. Neither horses nor riders looked up when I called out 'Hello!'.

I heard Daddy tell Mother later that a group of Boers had come in to surrender at the police station that afternoon. 'Poor buggers,' he said. And Mother didn't even chide him.

Some years passed before we moved back to Durban. Daddy stopped going to work – there was no longer work for him to go to, no money left to run the railway. It was during this time, a time of great depression across the whole Colony, that my little brother Will was born. Though she loved him, he was a great strain on Mother who was nearly forty by then.

Daddy turned down a new job with the railways because it was of lower status than the one he'd held in Ladysmith. Mother was furious, she couldn't keep a family together on the vegetables he grew, she said. They argued a lot, but always behind closed doors. The differences between them seemed to multiply. Mother would lose herself working in the garden and Daddy in his day-dreams. It was Oliver, darling, sainted Oliver who found work first, then me. When the Second World War broke out, Mother was frantic with worry about Oliver, but he was found to be unfit and could not enlist – perhaps because of all those childhood illnesses.

A few years after the war Mother began to show signs of rheumatoid arthritis. At first it was manageable, but then she could no longer garden, no longer cook. Then she could no longer bath or dress herself, no longer write, no longer hold a book. As her pain and disability increased she began needing more and more care, so I gave up my job as a dress-maker and nursed her. For years. My poor dear Walter. When he married me, he got my parents too.

After she died, I found a small suitcase I'd never seen before. It was made of sturdy red leather and measured only five by twelve by fifteen inches. Daddy said he'd never seen it before either, so I thought it wise to open it sometime when he was out visiting. The key, well that was easy, there was a small brass key tied on a scrap of faded blue fabric in among her under-wear. I'd always wondered about that key, but had known better than to ask.

Inside the suitcase was a magazine from the Royal Geographic Society dated 1892; a newspaper clipping about a woman explorer where Mother (I presume) had underlined just one sentence; ' "I could not endure a domestic lifestyle," said Miss Bird'; and a type-written note from the *Natal Herald* dated 13 August 1908, which read, 'Dear Mrs Knight. We regret to inform you, there are no vacancies for columnists at present.' My mother had entertained notions of being a writer and not one of us knew about it. There was also a thick white envelope addressed to Mr G. Knight, 13 Enfield Road, Durban, Port Natal, in Mother's hand. There was no stamp on the envelope, nor was it sealed. Inside was a letter dated 24 December 1892 – and the address given was Residencial da Opiniao do Porto, Lisbon. Mother must have stayed there when ship-wrecked.

'*My dear Gilbert*' I read with trepidation.

There is something I must tell you. It weighs heavily on my heart.
I thought I should be able to live with it. I thought it better not to
burden you with the truth, but there is something about surviving a
ship-wreck, something about another chance at life, that makes you
look at things differently.

I could not go on. I could not go on reading Mother's unsent letter. I did not want to know what had weighed so heavily on her heart. And why, if she had written it, had she not posted it? Why ever had she kept it? My always composed mother in a turmoil? My matter-of-fact mother with a dreadful secret?

I was always known as the rough, tough one – but in all truth I am a coward. Philemon was burning dry leaves in the fire pit at the bottom of the garden. It must have been May or June – the deciduous trees, jacaranda, leopard, golden trumpet, and the coral trees were all losing their leaves. I folded the pages carefully along the worn lines, and without looking down at the letter in my hands even once more, I slipped it back into its white envelope, and stood-up. Perhaps I was in shock. I walked across the lawn, past the violas, the mari-golds, past the sunflowers and the zinnias, past the purple cosmos growing beneath the leafless jacaranda and down the stones steps to the fire pit. Mother's secret blackened at the edges, puckered, and then burst into flames.

I suppose you could say I don't dare have a theory.

LITTLE GLADYS'S THEORY

I don't dabble in make-believe, I like facts, so I will only tell you what I know. The facts we have about my Grandmother Eleanor don't tell us anything about why she agreed to marry Gilbert, nor why he took ten years to propose. We don't know what she did in those years, though she'd clearly had enough of governess-ing by the end of it, and we only know a little of what Gilbert was up to. The only certain thing is that a correspondence ensued between them, and towards the end of 1892, he asked her to come out to Durban and marry him. She must still have been fond enough of him to say yes.

Gilbert, my Granddad, first went to South Africa as a member of the 60th Foot, King's Royal Rifle Corps. Why he joined the army was always a bit of a mystery. As far as I can tell, though he never confessed this to me himself, he had been involved in a fight with some chap who had insulted his girlfriend. The police were called, and Gilbert spent the night in jail. Next morning, unable to face his father, he fled to the army. Some months later, two hundred men were needed to go to Africa, to Isandhlwana, where the British Army were preparing to go into battle against the Zulus again. One February morning, their Colonel said: 'Let any men who wish to go, take one step to the front.'

Apparently, all eight hundred men stepped forward. Granddad said it was one of the most thrilling moments of his life. They sailed at the end of that same month ... ten thousand men in all. It was 1879.

The English made short work of the Zulus and troops were out of Zululand by September, except for some, including Granddad. And he was still there when the First Boer War broke out. Granddad survived Majuba, left as part of a small regiment at the bottom of the hill to guard lines of communication while the rest of the troops climbed to their deaths.

The following year, his sister died, and Granddad, who had been in and out of hospital with various diseases and was by this time sick too of being a soldier, wrote and asked his father to buy him out of the army, which his father duly did. He worked his passage home aboard a ship, and that is how he, Gilbert Knight came to be in Cowes, the summer of 1883.

Eleanor died before I was born. Though Granddad said very little about their meeting, I do remember him describing their first kiss, 'Aah! Nectar!' is what he said. But whatever he felt for Eleanor at the time, it wasn't sufficient to keep him in the home country. Africa was in his blood, and he left again just a few months later.

Once back in Natal, he took on all sorts of jobs. He was overseer of a road-making gang on Town Hill, Pietermaritzburg, and then a clerk for an accountant, before moving to Johannesburg. It was there he became engaged to a Miss Ferguson, but only for a short while. It seems he ended the arrangement somewhat abruptly on discovering something questionable about her moral standing. Perhaps because of this, he moved on to the Cape Colony, where he lived in quarters in the Castle, and worked as a civilian clerk for the military. Next he took a job in a law firm, again as a clerk. Eventually he returned to Natal, (preferring its clime and natives to the Cape's) where he became a clerk with the Natal Government Railway in Durban.

No guesses or theories. That's all I know.

SANDRA'S THEORY

Have you ever heard of Nellie Bly? She was so determined not to be confined to writing about gardening, fashion or food that she spent ten days in a mad house so she could write an article about it for the New York World in 1887. In 1889 she travelled around the world in seventy two days, six hours, eleven minutes and fourteen seconds – a record-breaking trip.

Have you heard of Isabella Lucy Bird? In 1889 her father gave her one hundred pounds and told her she could travel until she had spent it all. Isabella Lucy Bird visited India, Tibet, Persia, Kurdistan and Turkey. She stayed and stayed and stayed, adding to her income by writing travel articles. She reportedly said, this Isabella Lucy Bird, 'I cannot endure a domestic lifestyle'.

Have you heard of Mary French Sheldon? If not, Google her too. American born, she moved to London in 1876. In 1891 she left, not only to explore East Africa, but to explore it alone (being the 1890s – alone meant without other Europeans). 'For what good?' she was asked, and 'Whatever prompted you?' Her answer? 'My interests lie outside the limitations of women's legitimate province.'

My great-grandmother Eleanor Knight, nee Lewis, had heard of them. I have her red leather suitcase, and in it I found an old Royal Geographical Society magazine which had a piece on Isabella Lucy Bird; several newspaper articles by Nellie Bly about her round-the-world trip (which one of Eleanor's American cousins must have sent her) and an advertisement for Mary French Sheldon's book, entitled, *Sultan to Sultan: Adventures among the Masai and other tribes of east Africa.*

Perhaps I am guilty of projection, given my own love of travel. Perhaps I am guilty of making things up. I like to make things up. But my theory is this: Eleanor wanted to see the world, and Gilbert with all his stories of adventure, so far away across the seas in 'deepest-darkest-Africa', was the best ticket she had.

Letter to the Management

JULIA MARTIN

Of course you could say they are vermin. Sky rats. And yes, as you have pointed out several times, they make a mess. But at least you can't object to the noise. Cooing is a definitively restful sound. And the soft clack of a wing, the tap tap tap as they peck the grain, these surely disturb nobody.

For some time now the nurses have been feeding the pigeons in secret, against your orders. You must know this already. We all do. That every day one or two women are risking their jobs for my mother. You've probably also guessed that I'm the one who buys the food. When it runs out, she calls and says, 'Please buy more birdfood. There are some angry birds looking at me.'

My number is the only one she ever calls. Most times she forgets I'm her daughter. At ninety, her memory has retreated to a misty place where just a few clear images remain. Walking in the long grass of the hill with her father. Climbing the mango tree with her best friend Cyril. Opening the aviary door one evening and letting her mother's prized flock of yellow canaries all fly out and away.

Why am I telling you this? I need to speak to you really, but frankly the idea makes me nervous, and perhaps if I write it down, you'll see where I'm coming from. About the pigeons. And about my mother. I've come to see that the fact of her eroded memory does not make her less intelligent or imaginative or sensitive than she ever was. What it does mean is that she no longer possesses the comfort of remembering. Everything takes place in the bright glare of the present moment without past or future. Everything takes place in a narrow bed with the cot sides up, in a frail old body that can no longer climb trees or mountains, or even walk, thin legs strapped to the physio cushion to prevent displacement of the hip. Hour after hour, year after year.

Sometimes I try to imagine it. Throughout the day, I hear the intercom from the corridor, and the scary wails of the neighbours' dementia. Tired nurses come and go, wash and dress me. Bring pallid food on a tray. Some of them steal things. Some chat. Some are cruel to me, especially at night. I try to imagine it, but really I don't have the courage. My mother on the other hand (who lived her life, I must explain, as a strong and loving woman, a teacher, an artist, bright and resourceful) is devastatingly articulate about what she is now experiencing. She talks about the utter loneliness. The powerlessness. The fear.

And then there are the doves and pigeons. They come to her balcony for the food, and she watches them all day from her bed as the light moves through the leaves of the syringa tree. Rock pigeons, cinnamon doves, turtle doves. Many have damaged feet, toes missing from the threads that bind themselves around their claws. Solomon, her favourite old bastard, as she calls him, has only one foot but he still manages to get to the food first. My mother loves to tell me about him and the other birds. Their squabble and strut, the ruthless etiquette of their eating, the markings that make each one distinct, the flash of iridescence on an outstretched wing in the sun. When I feed them in the early morning on my way to work, she smiles and says, 'I wish you could see what you look like! All those birds flying around you. And the light.'

Today I had more time than usual and managed to entice one badly injured rock pigeon into her room and caught it so that I could unpick the twine from its feet. The threads were already biting deep into the flesh, and unwinding them took a while. But it made my mother happy, and the pigeon did not resist. It lay quietly on my lap and watched the movement of my hands with its red-rimmed eye. Finally the toes were free and it could walk again. It walked out of the room through the sliding door and flew away.

I realise now that I must have left some crushed mealies on the floor, because about an hour ago she called. Her voice was shaking, angry. The tears were close and she sounded frightened. She said, 'They've told me I can't feed the birds! It's Management, Mrs D. She came and shouted at me. She was very cross. She told me they make a mess.' There was a long pause, and I could hear her breathing coming fast and uneven. Then slowly, deliberately, she said, 'You see, darling, I just can't think what I'd do without those pigeons.'

Do I have to say more? There are pictures of the Pope in the corridors, so perhaps I could remind you of St Francis, or even the Holy Dove. Or I could talk about wildness, and the joy of the living world. Perhaps the simple truth is that the doves and pigeons are her friends. At the end of a long life, so much has been lost. But the birds still come and go, and she can still care for them.

So I told my mother not to worry. I promised that we'd carry on feeding them anyway, and that I would explain to you why. She really needs those vermin birds. While she is caught, they fly.

The Dream of Cats is All About Mice

ALEX SMITH

Hilm il-'utaat kullu firaan

The radio played, but that it did all night as usual, simply to add voices to an empty home. What woke him was the sound of dripping water coming from the light bulb, splattering into a container lined with a towel. He cursed the rain because rain meant traffic worse than usual, and he had a presentation that day: a new campaign for a famous brand of soap. Of the first things he saw upon rousing himself from a stupor were an old Easter egg and a pair of golden awards won for a yeast campaign.

Imraan recalled that yesterday he had walked to, and then home from, the Alma Cafe, and unlocked the gate all with one hand. In his other hand he had a chicken thigh, one of three he'd bought from the café. The gate needed oiling, so when he pushed it, the hinges squealed. Now at that time, in a tree overhead, a cat, much disliked in the neighbourhood, was a second past leaping, and in response to the shriek of metal below, she looked, which meant by a near nothing of space, she missed her branch and when Imraan stepped through the gate, she landed, dazed, at his feet. She made a great act of being fearsome, and vaguely Imraan registered from the scars across her face that this was the creature people called 'the bird killer'.

The cat had been excommunicated from every good home in the neighbourhood. On account of his unpredictable state of mind, Imraan barely registered her, despite her hiss-and-growl posturing. Perhaps it was the wrong response, but something of the cat falling from the sky amused him enough to laugh and actually feel happy, which in itself was unusual. He pulled off a strip of chicken and tossed it into the path for the cat, before proceeding along a path of bricks flanked by grass.

Without giving the cat another thought, he walked up five stairs to the stoep and an arched doorway these days solidly barred by a heavy-duty security gate. All the windows of the Victorian cottage were barred too. He unlocked the security gate and locked it behind himself before finding the key to unlock the front door. So it was while he was standing in the cage between the two doors that he heard the sound of the cat, and when he turned to look, there she was, but the suddenness of his turn made her spring oddly to the side, and Imraan laughed again.

Imraan sensed an opportunity as it dawned on him that this was the infamous cat, the cat who could attack, the cat who had fallen from grace in good society. Imraan didn't care much for the good society of that street. He tore more chicken off the thigh that was his dinner, and then with boldness he did not expect of himself, he sank to his knees and held the piece of chicken through the security bars for the scarred cat. She was about half a metre away, and Imraan did not expect her to take the food from his hand, simply because the people around there had treated her so badly. It came as a great surprise when the cat came forward, purring, and ate out of his hand. Still stuck there between the bars and the door, Imraan, whose life had until that moment seemed a pit of bleakness, which he tried on a daily basis to deny, was delighted. He thought with a self-congrat-ulatory tinge and in the third person, as he always imagined himself the narrator of the re-enactment of the life of a young man: *Who ever knows what a cat thinks, but perhaps the young man's kindness was so refreshing, it dissolved all her defences, and brought out the best in the bird killer.*

The greatness of Imraan's delight was disproportionate to the actual event and he knew it. *A cat eating chicken is not such a cause for celebration, but for this young man, alone in the world, it became a great joy, and even greater, in fact, utterly breathtaking, when the cat slunk through the grill and joined him in the cage between the doors.*

As the sun set on Rosebank and Table Mountain beyond, Imraan and the cat crouched there, both eating chicken. So close to this loathed and feared cat, Imraan saw a side of her few ever saw. She was in fact graceful and beautiful. He wanted to stroke her, but such proximate affection did not suit either of their temperaments. Instead, overcome with emotion, he said, holding out his hand: 'I could kiss you.' He had no illusions about cats being able to under-stand English, but perhaps she understood his tone, because she blinked her eyes and purred more loudly.

She seemed an impossible cat to hate, and he wondered at the coldness of his neighbours, but then the chicken was all eaten and the special moment between them had to end. Imraan gave her the third thigh, and stood, and while she devoured it, he unlocked the door, and went into his home, and had no further thoughts of the cat, because once inside he was plagued with his usual worries.

In the kitchen a clock ticked heavily, the old fridge – empty of food other than various jars of pickles, preserves, jams, sauces, at least half of them purchased at farm stalls on various family road trips, opened, tasted and abandoned – rumbled. The place smelled of wet cat food although there had not been a bowl of cat food out for a long time. In a low drawer filled with things to forget, there were still pouches of Whiskas and Friskies, for a long-gone cat belonging to a long-gone family. The Whiskas and the Friskies lingered, as did the cardboard box shaped like an Easter egg, and filled with chocolates never eaten.

Imraan was not by tradition a man who celebrated Easter, but regardless of religious norms, children hate to be left out of festivities, especially when they involve chocolate. The egg might stay on the kitchen table for eternity, but the children he had bought it for were now living in another country, with their mother. It was printed with a scene of a happy sun and anthropomorphised chickens and chicks, all dressed in clothes and prancing through a meadow filled with flowers and eggs in yellow, red and turquoise. Every time he walked into the kitchen, Imraan saw that egg, and then the drawings and photographs stuck on the fridge door. One person, in one drawing, was wearing a striped T-shirt: between the stripes was written 'Barbie's best T-shirt'. Over the person in Barbie's best was written: 'I'm whistling for today, yesterday I didn't know how.'

He'd left all the aprons hanging on the hook behind the door leading to the yard, even though he never wore an apron, even if he did cook – and lately he couldn't be bothered to cook. He'd taken to eating breakfast cereal at meals other than breakfast, or takeaways or tinned food. There was a tin of Koo Pear Halves in Syrup on the table, and after washing the chicken grease off his fingers, he took out a tin opener.

Then he sat watching *Crimes That Shook Britain* on the Crime and Investigation channel. Something about the horror of it comforted him – that other people had worse disasters in their life. This night featured a family in a country town: a mother, father, and two daughters. The scenario hurt Imraan's memory. Everything in the re-enactment was so ideal, but by virtue of the channel, it would have to change for the very worst, along the lines of his philosophy of the moment: the glass is already broken. On his yellow sofa, Imraan bit into a pear half as the father took his daughters in their gingham uniforms to school, and the voice of a narrator noted that the girls could not possibly realise how in a matter of hours their lives would alter. Father went to work, mother fetched the girls in the afternoon, and because it was sunny, mother and daughters and their poodle went for a walk along a country lane. There again everything turned on a detail, a matter of position along the lane.

Imraan was appalled at the story. *At the programme's end, the young man felt a kinship with the father, for he knew something of what that father felt. Although his circumstances were totally different, far less shocking, more mundane, the young man knew the feeling of sudden bewildering loss: loss that comes like lightning, and over the tiniest detail, and destroys everything.* Unoriginal perhaps, but it was impossible for him not to wonder obsessively over what he had done in this life or a past life, to deserve such blinding loss. No answer, there was simply no answer.

Night was stubborn, and would not pass. Imraan took a Murakami novel called *Dance Dance Dance* to bed, but fell asleep while reading, and then he woke at one in the morning with the light on and the radio playing too loudly. So he turned off the light, turned down the radio, and plugged in his electric blanket for some warmth. But now that he was aiming for sleep, it eluded him. He considered reading again, but knew he must work the next day; he needed to come up with a scintillating TV advert about margarine, and should make an attempt at rest if not sleep. To sell margarine he had to become margarine, he had to inhabit margarine, to write from margarine's perspective, but he didn't want to be margarine. *Margarine was beginning to give the young man suicidal ideation.* He did not sleep until six – half an hour before the alarm sounded.

It would have been an ordinary day of margarine if he hadn't opened and closed the front door, opened and closed the security gate, descended the five stairs, and halfway along the path come across 'the bird killer'. Imraan stopped and she looked at him with astonishing green eyes. *He certainly had not expected her return, and it seemed to the young man that she was telling him stories with her eyes, of past adventures and battles; for sure she'd been through many: the scars on her forehead and raggedy left ear were proof of it.*

'Battle Cat,' Imraan said, 'I'll call you Battle Cat.' He would have liked to give her something more to eat, but he was in a hurry, the margarine people were expecting him to call, and it seemed the cat was also in a hurry. She'd seen a mantis, and sprang about with mildly hilarious glee, caught it and then darted off into the bushes, the insect in her mouth. Finally she disappeared up a tree, then over the wall. *The young man chuckled, and was left with a definite sense of magic, because Battle Cat was impossibly elegant in all her movements, even the mad ones, perhaps especially those – the acrobatic contortions of a happy hunter.*

The day of margarine went by surprisingly easily because of Battle Cat; she had brightened Imraan's view of everything, and the possibility of finding her again in his garden made him happy. This even though the margarine people had rejected his suggestions and his boss, who once adored him for winning the agency an award at Cannes, had told him he was losing it, and some woman had practically reversed into him, and then ranted at him when it was her fault in the first place. Tuna would make a change from the chicken he'd eaten every night for probably more than a week. On the way home he bought two tins of tuna from the Alma Cafe – one for himself and one for Battle Cat, even though he half expected never to see her again. And, indeed, there was no sign of her when he arrived home. Still he scooped the tuna into a white saucer and left it on the stoep for her, but near the lounge window, across from the yellow sofa, so that he could see, while watching the Crime and Investigation channel, if she came. With his shoes off and his feet bare, he ate his tuna directly from the tin, and sat through all of the first part of a series called *Mobsters*. It was during a fascinating three a.m. rerun of 'Women Behind Bars' – Imraan had finished his tuna and was eating tinned peaches – that she meowed. She called him! Whoever the incarcerated woman on DSTV was, she was nowhere near as real and as happy-making as Battle Cat. In his bare feet, T-shirt and shorts, Imraan ran to the entrance hall, unlocked the door, the security gate, and even though the slate tiles of the stoep were icy and it was chilly out, and drizzling, he went to greet the cat. She was eating the tuna in anxious gulps with her teeth showing, and some of the salty fish flew off the saucer and scattered around the rim. She was purring, though, and Imraan took that to mean something akin to friendship.

Imraan wanted to touch her, but didn't want to disturb her eating, and then it was too late: the saucer was empty and she scampered back into the night. *That was when the young man first appreciated the difference between cats and men, and the way they experience the same things. That gave him a jolt, 'That's it!' He incorporated the epiphany into the margarine advert with great success. So the cat had inspired him, and for a young man going clean and so through an inspiration drought, that meant a lot to him: it was close to saving his life.*

'Fucking brilliant,' his boss said of the cat concept. 'I was about to tell you to take a long sabbatical, but now I think I'll put you on the Lighthouse Bread account.'

191

That evening, after a stellar meeting with the margarine people, Imraan returned home with two tins of John West Salmon for the cat that had made him laugh, and had inspired him and rejuvenated his career.

The garage door creaked upwards. He parked. He hummed, he was feeling cheery, it had been a day of good decisions. In the garage darkness, he found his way to the door that led to the garden. Soon as he opened it, the twilight came in, and he wandered out. 'Battle Cat,' he called. 'Hello,' he said cheerily. She was not there, but he was in such a fine mood that he determined he should find her. The salmon tins had those easy to remove peel-open lids. He opened one tin of salmon and bandied it towards the breeze, hoping the cat would be close and would catch a whiff of it. Like a fool really, he held the can up towards the trees and the sky beyond. 'Hellooo ... Battle Cat....' Battle Cat did not appear, so next Imraan unlocked the garden gate, and tin in hand went out into the street, calling for her.

It was the first bad decision of the day. There were neighbours positioned along the road, watching Imraan, clutching his tins of John West Salmon, one open. 'Battle Cat,' he called, anxious now. His heart began to race, and his palms to sweat, but he continued his quest to proffer salmon to this cat they called 'the bird killer'.

In time, she came, and not alone; perhaps sensing the hostility of the neighbours, she'd come with an ally. A tom cat, in fact a well-liked tom cat in the 'hood. They sauntered towards Imraan. He went down on his haunches, and since there was now a guest, he opened the second tin – it had been destined for his dinner, but Imraan wanted to show his beady-eyed neighbours what it meant to be hospitable. *The young man wanted to remind his neighbours of that quote, was it Whitman? Be not inhospitable to strangers, lest they be angels in disguise.*

Battle Cat and the tom ate with mild gusto between mews and purrs and a little slinking. Yes, Battle Cat, for the first time, walked up to Imraan and rubbed her cheek gently against his hand – not for long, but for long enough, and he felt some electric recognition of spirit and was smitten. *It had been too long since the young man had allowed any kind of closeness into his life.*

Imraan's mobile phone rang, and either it was the noise or Imraan's sudden movement to answer, but Battle Cat and the tom fled.

'What's that commotion?' It was his Aunt Faizah on the phone.

Imraan explained he had befriended a cat. 'She's a beauty,' he said, perhaps with too much awe in his voice. 'So funny, and enchanting, Aunty Faizah, she really makes me laugh and she's soft and gentle ... and inspiring ...'

'Stop it, Imraan!'

'What?'

'You're talking about a cat. A cat! A filthy stray.'

'She's not filthy, Aunty Faizah ... you must see her eyes, and at the back of her head, the hair almost curls. I think I might take her in, you know, give her a home.'

'*Hilm il-'utaat kullu firaan.*' Aunty Faizah's voice was despondent.

'And that means?'

'The dream of cats is all about mice, Imraan.' Aunty Faizah tut-tutted. 'I wish you had a one-track mind.... Sex, Imraan, don't you miss it?'

'Aunty!' Imraan put shock in his tone even though he was no prude, quite the opposite. Other women in his family were more traditional, but Aunty Faizah worked as a features writer for *Cosmopolitan* and spoke openly of multiple orgasms.

'When last did you go on a date?'

There was no answer.

'What you need is a woman, not a filthy stray cat!'

'Actually for a creature that lives on the streets, she's remarkably clean.'

After work the next day, Imraan bought a whole fresh linefish, some for his dinner and some for Battle Cat.

Once home, he rolled out the portable braai, which had not been used since his split from the woman he loved, who had left for Amsterdam taking the children he loved and wished were his, but were not biologically his. He had no claim to them, and he had screwed up, after all. 'My wife and my children,' he said, absently thinking of the travesty of change (*Why do things have to change? wondered the young man*) as he cooked the fish with Battle Cat looking on.

Stars came out and a nearly half moon.

Sitting at a metal table on the porch, Imraan and the cat ate the yellowtail until only foil and bones remained. Then, while Imraan drank his way through two bottles of wine, one white, one red, Battle Cat sat in the chair opposite him. When Imraan finally rose to go to bed, Battle Cat followed him to the door. Then sensing the pleasant evening was over, she disappeared away into bushes, but after Imraan had locked himself behind the security gate, Battle Cat reappeared. She looked in through the bars of the security gate, down the hallway tiled in black and white and lined with bookshelves.

'Come on, come in,' Imraan said, and she did, and Imraan locked the front door, and together they found their way to his bed. Imraan did not bother to undress. He collapsed and when he woke, feeling the rough effects of too much wine, Battle Cat was there, on his chest, sleeping. He studied her features and scars until his sniff caused her to open her eyes. It was some comfort to wake up with a friend, but Aunty Faizah was right: a cat could not be what a cat was not.

Still, Imraan was ready to open his house to this creature because he liked her company and admired her very much. He sniffed again, and Battle Cat was disturbed: in a blink, she'd jumped off the bed and run out of the room. She found her way to the open window in the lounge and vanished.

In the week following the braai, Imraan put out a plate of tuna every night. The first night Battle Cat came and ate the tuna, but only when Imraan was not there. Still, it made him happy to know she was in his life and not completely gone.

The second night she did not come.

On the third day, Imraan glimpsed her walking along his wall, but when she saw him, she ran. He could not understand her behaviour. *The young man was bewildered.* What had he done wrong this time? He took it for granted everything was always his fault, but what was it?

The next week, the week of his thirty-eighth birthday, Imraan, quite distraught at being so abandoned and rejected, bought John West Salmon and tried that, but Battle Cat did not return. *The young man was confounded, hurt, disproportionately devastated, and then he felt ludicrous – how could I be so pathetic to be so infatuated with a vanishing cat?*

The kettle clicked off and the radio was playing, filling the home with some near humanity, and the clock said it was time to move on and into the traffic in order to arrive and dazzle with the presentation to the soap company. Battle Cat had never returned; Imraan hankered for her, once glimpsed her hurrying across the road – she saw him, but did not bother to pause. He sometimes left food for her, but never again did he eat with her or sleep with her. It was an unsatisfactory ending. And that was how she inspired his most successful campaign to date: when life around you doesn't go as you hope, you can always count on Lighthouse Bread for a happy ending. People related. Imraan glanced at the pair of golden awards won at Cannes. In advertising circles, he had become famous and envied. But those who thought his life was glamorous knew nothing. *The young man thought of Battle Cat. If not in hers, in his life then, their meeting had been a significant event.*

Shortlisted for the UJ Debut Prize for creative writing | 2017
Winner of the NIHSS Award for fiction by a single author | 2018

The Fisherman

JOLYN PHILLIPS

Andrea gets up with a sense of purpose. It is early, so early that the moon is the only thing that reflects on the calm waves. But Andrea's mind is already active with thoughts of the harbour, the concrete bareness of it. The harbour with the dolosse that look like giant hammers, stacked on top of each other to barricade the sea from pushing forward. Those bloody seagulls that shit everywhere. The revolting smell of sea guts that she loves. How here in Gansbaai the sea is not blue as in the pictures. It is grey and when the sea is moody with cramps, she builds up foam that looks like someone threw a box of OMO washing powder in the sea, so that it might push the soap suds forwards to the shore.

Andrea has to get ready for work. She puts on her three pairs of socks first, followed by sweatpants. Then she puts on a T-shirt and a polo-neck jersey over it and finally her green oilskin dungarees and the black balaclava she knitted for today's occasion. When she is finished, she goes to the kitchen and takes her lunchbox which used to be an ice-cream tub that read *Country Fresh Vanilla Ice Cream* on it. But the sticky label is now withered. Four slices of bread with margarine is all she needs. That is what her Pappa used to have in his lunchbox.

When Andrea gets to the harbour she knows she is two hours early. The boats usually come into the harbour round about eight,

197

but she doesn't want to miss the skipper. She is only here for one reason. She has come to ask for her father's work and she won't leave until he says yes. Although the smell of fish maize stings in your nose, it is a blessed smell for the men and women working at the factory and for her. Every day they wait for the early-morning hoeter to sing through the streets of Blompark to wake them up to catch the can-bus so that they can go work at the fish factory. But Andrea has never wanted to work at the can factory or by the label store. Since she was very young she wanted to be a fisherman, like Pappa.

Every day when Pappa came from the sea she waited for him on the stoep to help pull off his toboots and oilskin. He would always let her check his pockets for loose change or, if he was in a good mood, he would bring home bokkoms to be enjoyed with dry bread and a cup of coffee.

Andrea notices a boat coming into the harbour. She notices how the seagulls are becoming restless, swarming like fleas towards the boat. She gets up quickly. She thinks she needs to get to the skipper before those bleddie seagulls. She hurries along the pier, careful not to slip as a member of the crew jumps off the boat to tie the boat. It must have been a bad day at sea, she thinks. She can see the skipper is particularly moody today. He and his manne are busy off-loading equipment and some of their personal belongings, not fish like other days. But she walks over and taps him on his shoulder.

'Ja meisiekint, what do you want? I don't want to buy fish.'

'Oh no, Skipper, I am not here to sell fish. I am here to ask for my father's job.'

'Look, I don't think there is place for you here.'

Andrea wants to tell the skipper that she wants to be a fisherman just like her Pappa. How she has dreamt of all the sea stories Pappa told her and the people he met when they went to Mosselbaai to catch pilchards for the fish factory. When she dreamt Pappa's stories she was one of the men at sea. She was all grown up with a beard just like Pappa's and she had on a balaclava for the cold and toboots to match with her green oilskin, just like she is wearing today. She can be like Pappa pulling in the nets through the wind and storm. She knows what a boat feels like when it is grinding through the waves. She can smoke her BB tobacco pipe and she has a strong stomach, she is used to the smell of the salt air and fish guts.

Her Pappa took her with him every Saturday to the harbour when the fishing boats lay on their sides at anchor. She and Pappa sat on the jetty with the tyres around it and listened to the seagulls' terrible singing. They sat there with their fishing string and their rooiaas and hoped for a harder to bite or, if they were lucky, a red roman fish. Pappa taught her everything about fish and water. He gave her first Okapi knife and fisher's needle to sew up the holes in the fishing nets. She was only twelve, but by then she was just as good as Pappa. She can do this job better than any of these manne still wet behind the ears calling themselves fishermen. I know the sea, Skipper, she wants to say. I know the sea, even though you are not even looking at me and acting restless, ready to leave the harbour as soon as possible.

'Look,' says Andrea, 'don't tell me that the sea is no place for me. I was born here. I am made from this salt I taste on my chapped lips, and my hands have caught fish for as long as I can remember. You won't be sorry. Pappa said I must get my sea legs, that you will understand our situation. Skipper mos know about Pappa? The sugar took him pretty bad and ate his leg. The sugar took him from us last year. We are eight children. I have to wear the pants in the house now. I wouldn't ask you for a job if my grasmasjien didn't die on me last week. I can work for myself, no problem, but I am running out of options.'

The skipper looks at Andrea. She can see she has his attention now. He waves away one of his men and looks uncomfortable. He begins to scratch his beard like he wants to say something but he doesn't know how. He is going to tell me to go away. Even after everything I have told him, Andrea thinks. Better pull up your pants, girlie. This may be your last chance.

'I know it is not your business. But I cannot catch enough fish to make it till the end of the week. You know with the permits and laws. Five fishes a day is not going to pay for everything,' Andrea says, cool and calm. She is looking the skipper right in the eye now. Man to man. She will not let him ignore her or dismiss her, the way he would chase away a thieving seagull.

'Yes but ... child but–' the skipper stutters.

'Yes, I understand that you have never appointed someone like me. Is it my hair? I will cut it if necessary. I wouldn't ask you if I wasn't in the red. I know about trying to hit blood out of a rock. I have been a deckman for Oubaas Tollie when Pappa worked for him. Pappa said you and your father are good people.'

'Why don't you work by the fish factory? This is no place for someone like you.'

'Skipper, I can't work at the fish factory. I wasn't born to be a fish packer. You should know what it is like being called to catch fish.'

'Yes but–'

'I know you think that I am crazy, but just give me a chance. You will see. Didn't you buy fish from me last week? You yourself told me that you haven't seen such good gevlekte fish since Oom Day last vlekked fish. Well, Skipper, I am his daughter and fishing is the oldest story I know. So can I start tomorrow?'

'Look, if you interrupt me one more time I swear your ears will burn. I don't mind you working for me.' The skipper dropped his voice now so that only Andrea could hear, 'But you have come at the wrong time. When last have you seen my boat on the water?' Skipper was looking in the direction of his men busy talking to each other. To the skipper they seemed cheerful, but he knew that once he had spoken to this girl he was going to tell them the same thing he was about to tell her.

'*Runtu*, my boat, is broken like your father's leg. There is nothing I can do any more. I am selling the boat to the owner of the fish factory and then I'm going to live with my children in Cape Town. I can't help you, kintjie. We are both in the same boat here. It is by God's grace that I was out at sea today. I hoped we would be able to catch something so that I could give the men a little something as pay. But the motor cut out and we barely made it back to port. She needs a new engine, a new rudder. Wood in the stern is rotten. Her GPS doesn't work any more. Truth is, I can't afford to keep her. Not with the government quotas on how much we can catch and when and what. This was *Runtu*'s last day at sea. I'm sorry.'

Andrea has nothing to say. She feels like a giant wave has smashed all the oxygen from her body and now all she can do is sink sink sink. Will she drown? She watches the skipper walk over to his bakkie where his men are all inside waiting for him. They drive off and Andrea still can't move. Those men, she thinks as the bakkie disappears past the boom and car park, like her they will have to scavenge with the seagulls tomorrow. These seagulls at this harbour have no shame, shitting everywhere like they do. They never do an honest day's work or know what it is to have hope taken from you when there is so little hope left.

Will I drown? Andrea thinks again, looking at the skipper's boat. Soon to be firewood or used to take tourists out. Andrea puts down her rucksack and unzips it. She takes out some fishing line and a hook and some rooiaas that was left from yesterday and walks over to the jetty. No, she will not drown. Not today. She sits herself down and throws her line into the water.

The Good Housekeeping Magazine Quiz

JO-ANN BEKKER

1. Your husband's First Big Love is crossing an ocean to come
   and visit him after thirty years. Would you say:
   a. 'I've got so much work to do I can't talk about this now.'
   b. 'How did you get in touch with her anyway?'
   c. 'What does she want? To introduce you to your love child?'
   d. 'She's not staying here.'
   e. All of the above.

2. Your husband's FBL has booked a week's accommodation
   in your town. You will be away at a conference for five of
   these nights. Would you:
   a. Say: 'I've got so much work I can't think about this now.'
   b. Tell your best friend.
   c. Tell your sister.
   d. Tell a tableful of mutual friends who all take it in turns
      to cross-examine your husband with glee.
   e. All of the above.

3. Your husband tells a tableful of friends that he sees FBL's
   visit as the biggest threat to his marriage in twenty-five years.

His worst fear is that he will be attracted to her. Would you:

a. Say: 'Well I will be away at a conference that week so it's up to you.'

b. Say: 'Just make sure you don't rock our son's emotional stability. Remember he is in matric.'

c. Take comfort in the horrified looks on your friends' faces as they sing your praises and call the imposter names.

d. Turn cold when you see how serious your husband is when he says this.

e. Collect a pile of dirty plates to take to the kitchen.

4. Your husband has photographs in his studio waiting for FBL's visit. They are pictures she gave him when she was seventeen. She is standing against a wall in baggy pants and a long-sleeved white T-shirt. Her hair is down in one and she is holding it up in another. She looks young and sweet and beautiful. Do you feel:

a. Threatened.

b. Threatened.

c. Threatened.

d. Threatened.

e. All of the above.

5. Next to the photographs is a copy of a story he told her every night before they went to sleep. A story about a frog which he illustrated at art school. Do you:

a. Think: 'Well he tried to tell me the same story but I kept pointing out the non sequiturs and asking him questions.'

b. Think: 'They spoke different languages so maybe this was their way of communicating.'

c. Remember a publisher telling him the story did not have a focus.

d. Skim through it again and notice how many babies the frogs had.

e. Go back to your desk and try to work.

6. FBL is arriving in a week. Do you tell yourself:

a. I could leave this town and get a full-time job. I could have a whole new life on my own.

b. I could rent a little house near a surf break. My older son would come and stay with me in his holidays.

c. I could move to a city. My younger son would come and stay with me in his holidays.

d. But after a while I would start looking for a new partner. Would I find the same connection, the same contentment?

e. I'll never have the same shared history with anyone.

7. It is your silver wedding anniversary three days before FBL arrives. Do you:

a. Go out for dinner and speak frankly and at length about your relationship and how threatened you feel about FBL's visit.

b. Listen to him say he is as nervous as you.

c. Notice how thin he has become.

d. Wonder if he's deliberately lost weight to look more youthful.

e. Order another glass of wine.

8. FBL arrives in two days. Do you have:

a. Excruciating neck pain.

b. No appetite.

c. Pain in your right nipple.

d. Diarrhoea.

e. All of the above.

9. FBL arrives tomorrow. Your husband says he thinks he'll go and have afternoon tea with her at her guest house. Do you:

   a. Say: 'For god's sake don't go rushing over there, wait for her to settle in and contact you.'

   b. Realise that you are just delaying the inevitable.

   c. Check his phone while he is in the shower and see he never read out the last line of her message: Hopefully see you very soon.

   d. Not mention that you checked his phone.

   e. Take anti-inflammatories for your neck.

10. It is the night before FBL arrives. Do you initiate sex and go down on your husband because:

    a. You want to.

    b. The tension is killing you.

    c. It might be the last time you want to.

    d. He won't be able to say he's not getting this at home.

    e. You might never make love with him again.

11. It is the morning of FBL's arrival. Your husband has spent the previous week planting fifty trees in the garden. He has tidied the lounge. He has left to bring FBL to your house for tea. Do you:

    a. Busy yourself printing out reports for your work trip the next day.

    b. Go to the loo.

    c. Take another anti-inflammatory for your neck.

    d. Wear ordinary clothes and no make-up because really you couldn't be bothered and perhaps this shows that you are not threatened.

    e. Put a load of laundry in the washing machine.

12. As you are reading the Sunday paper at the kitchen table, your husband's car pulls up outside. You get up and open the front door. Do you:

    a. See a heavy middle-aged woman. See your husband look at you with don't-worry-this-is-not-the-girl-I-used-to-know eyes.

    b. Welcome her, make tea, ask to see pictures of her daughters, show her pictures of your sons.

    c. Notice her tight clothes, gelled hair, new leather boots. Notice her even-toned skin. Notice the tension around her mouth. Notice how freaked out she becomes by a mosquito bite.

    d. See her relax and become more animated. Hear her similar views on child rearing to yours. See the way she looks at your husband. See the way he looks at you. See how she is beautiful at certain angles. Feel the tension in your own mouth.

    e. All of the above – so you excuse yourself to hang up laundry.

13. You, your husband, your younger son and Yael go to a seaside restaurant for lunch. Do you:

    a. Insist your husband drives Yael so you can give your son a driving lesson.

    b. Tell your son Yael is a friend of his father's from Israel. Watch with pride as he behaves charmingly throughout lunch.

    c. Talk Yael through the menu.

    d. Notice how she turns her back on your husband and faces you for most of the meal.

    e. Notice how difficult she finds it to chew.

14. Your husband and Yael arrive home from the restaurant one hour after your son and you. Do you:
    a. Let them talk some more on the stoep while you pack for your trip.
    b. Give Yael some ointment for her mosquito bite.
    c. Tell her it was nice to meet her. Mean it.
    d. Watch her say: 'Thank you for all this.' Her hands raised and open, indicating what?
    e. Tell her you'll be away for the week and your husband will be very busy looking after your son. Wonder if you should have said that.

15. After your husband takes Yael back to her guest house do you:
    a. Think about what she's done: chosen to leave her two daughters, husband, family and friends and come to South Africa to find closure with a boyfriend she knew thirty years ago.
    b. Realise she was vague about whether she was still living with her husband.
    c. Think about what she said: 'This is a present I am giving myself for my fiftieth birthday.'
    d. Feel her pain.
    e. Think about what she said about her siblings. How they are so jealous of her. How she was in therapy to deal with their hostility. Wonder what she told her therapist about your husband.

16. When your husband returns home, he makes you tea and you sit down to talk. Does he tell you:
    a. Yael told him she would have come to visit even if he had

tried to dissuade her. She had re-read all his letters and found one where he told her he loved her.
b. She wasn't interested in doing much tourist stuff.
c. All she wanted to do was go over the past.
d. He is grateful for how warm you were to her. She said she was grateful too.
e. He will wait for her to initiate the next contact. He will look after your son while you are away. He will probably meet her for lunch a few times.

17. It is five nights later and you have just arrived home from your demanding conference. You spoke to your husband once during the week and he said FBL's visit was going well and she seemed to be happier. Now your husband walks through the door with a pink rose he was given at a relative's funeral. He gives you the rose, you put it in water and ask about his week. His face has a crumpled expression you've never seen before. Do you ask him:
a. If it was a difficult week.
b. Whether FBL wanted more from him at every meeting.
c. Whether they had a lot of physical contact.
d. Whether they had sex.
e. All of the above.

AUTHORS

JAYNE BAULING

Jayne Bauling is best known for her YA novels which have won several awards, and two are DBE-approved school set-works. She has twice been shortlisted for the Commonwealth Short Story Prize; her short stories and poems have been published in a number of anthologies, as well as in print and online literary journals. She is also a regular contributor of YA stories to FunDza Literacy Trust, and lives in White River, Mpumalanga.

JO-ANN BEKKER

Jo-Ann Bekker's *Asleep Awake Asleep* (2019) is the most recent Modjaji story collection. Bekker is a prize winning journalist who began writing short fiction after working as a newspaper reporter for many years. She has an MA in Creative Writing from Rhodes University. Her short fiction has been published in *New Contrast, Volume 1 Brooklyn, Aerodrome, Type/Cast, Problem House Press* and *The Drum* literary magazine. She was born in East London and lives in Knysna.

TINASHE CHIDYAUSIKU

Tinashe Chidyausiku is young female writer born and raised in Zimbabwe. She graduated from Africa University to become a creative writer of diverse works from stories to songs. She has been writing since the age of seven till present with the encouragement and inspiration of her father, a writer in his own right. She is a kindergarten teacher who uses expressive arts such as theatre to help small children develop confidence.

MELISSA DE VILLIERS

Melissa de Villiers is a writer and editor. Her short story collection, *The Chameleon House*, was nominated for the Frank O'Connor International Short Story award. Born and bred in Makhanda, Eastern Cape, Melissa now divides her time between London and Singapore.

COLLEEN HIGGS

As well as being a writer, Colleen is also a publisher, she started the independent southern African feminist press, Modjaji Books in 2007. She lives in Cape Town with her daughter, a cat and two dogs. Her published works include a short story collection, *Looking for Trouble* (2012), and two poetry collections *Half Born Woman* (2004) and *Lava Lamp Poems* (2011).

SANDRA HILL

Sandra Hill is a writer, editor and writing facilitator. She also guides on the Rim of Africa mega trail, and works at an indie bookshop. Her debut collection of short stories, *UnSettled and other stories*, published in 2015, won the SALA Nadine Gordimer Short Story Award in 2016. Her poetry has been published in local journals and anthologies including New Contrast, and The Sol Plaatje EU Poetry Anthology.

LAURI KUBUITSILE

Lauri Kubuitsile is a multiple award winning author of more than thirty books. Her novel, *The Scattering* (Penguin 2016), won Best International Fiction Book 2017 at the Sharjah International Book Fair and was recommended by the prestigious Walter Scott Prize for Historical Fiction in the UK. North American rights have been bought by Waveland Press (USA). Her second historical novel *But Deliver Us from Evil* was published by Penguin this year. She lives in Botswana.

SARAH LOTZ

Sarah Lotz is a novelist and screenwriter with a fondness for the macabre and fake names. Among other things she writes urban horror novels under the name S.L Grey with author Louis Greenberg, and a YA series with her daughter Savannah under the pseudonym Lily Herne. Her latest novel is *Missing Person*.

RENEILWE MALATJI

Reneilwe Malatji was born in Modjaji Village in 1968. She grew up in Turfloop Township, in the northern part of South Africa. She has a post graduate diploma in Journalism and an MA in Creative Writing from Rhodes University. She is currently working on a doctorate at the University of the Western Cape and is a lecturer at the University of Limpopo. She has an adult son. Her first book, *Love Interrupted* won two prizes, the 2014 Nadine Gordimer SALA award and the 2014 Aidoo-Snyder Book award (a US prize).

JULIA MARTIN

Julia Martin is a professor in the English Department at the University of the Western Cape. The situation described in 'Letter to the Management' is further developed in her recent book, *The Blackridge House: A Memoir* (Jonathan Ball, 2019).

WAME MOLEFHE

Wame Molefhe is a freelance writer from Botswana. Her writings are published in journals, anthologies, and online. She has had two short story collections published. *Go Tell the Sun* was first published by Modjaji Books in 2011.

ISABELLA MORRIS

Isabella Morris is a teacher, award-winning writer, ghostwriter, and editor. She is the author of four full-length books, and several short stories that have been translated and appeared in numerous publications, locally and internationally. She is currently working on her PhD in creative writing (UKZN) focussing on decolonised trauma theory, and lives in Alexandria, Egypt where she teaches English.

JOLYN PHILLIPS

Jolyn Phillips was born and bred in Blompark, Gansbaai. Her collection of short stories, *Tjieng Tjang Tjerries and other stories*, published in 2016 was shortlisted for the 2017 UJ prize for best Debut and won the NIHSS Prize for Best Fiction by a single author in 2018. In July 2017, her debut collection of Afrikaans poetry, *Radbraak*, was published; it was shortlisted for the Elizabeth Eybers Prize (2018) and won the UJ Prize for the 2018 best Debut. She currently lectures in the Afrikaans Department at the University of Johannesburg and is working on a PhD in Creative Writing (UWC).

ARJA SALAFRANCA

Arja Salafranca's fiction is collected in her debut collection, *The Thin Line* (2010), longlisted for the Wole Soyinka Award in 2012. She has published three collections of poetry, *A Life Stripped of Illusions* (1995), which received the Sanlam Award, *The Fire in which we Burn* (2000); and *Beyond Touch* (2015) which was a co-winner of the SALA Poetry Award. Her next book is a collection of creative non-fiction to be published by Modjaji in 2020. She lives in Johannesburg. http://arjasalafranca.blogspot.com

ALEX SMITH

Alex Smith lives in Cape Town with her writer-archaeologist partner, two sons, a couple of dogs and a garden full of cacti. She tutors grammar and novel writing for a college based in New Zealand, and has had five novels and many short stories published.

MEG VANDERMERWE

Meg is a Senior Lecturer in Creative Writing and English Literature at the University of the Western Cape. Her novel, *Zebra Crossing* (2013) was selected by the Cape Times as one of the ten best South African books published in 2013 and chosen for the *Guardian* newspaper, as one of the Top 10 books about migrants. Her new novel, *The Woman of the Stone Sea/Die Vrou Van Die Klippesee*, (Umuzi, 2019) is set in a West Coast fishing village and features an IsiXhosa water maiden (umamlambo) and a local crayfish fisherman.

MAKHOSAZANA XABA

Makhosazana Xaba is an anthologist, biographer-in-the-making, essayist, short story writer and poet. She is currently a Research Associate at the Wits Institute for Social and Economic Research (WiSER) and a patron of the Johannesburg Review of Books. In 2019 she published her third poetry collection *The Alkalinity of Bottled Water* and edited *Our Words, Our Worlds: Writing on Black South African Women Poets 2000-2018*. She holds an MA in Creative Writing (with distinction).

The stories in *Fool's Gold* were originally published in the Modjaji Books' titles listed below. The stories in the collection are arranged according to date of publication.

"Botswana Rain" by Wame Molefhe from *Go Tell The Sun* (2011)

"The Red Earth" by Meg Vandermerwe from *This Place I Call Home* (2010)

"The Thin Line" by Arja Salafranca from *The Thin Line* (2010)

"Stains Like a Map" by Jayne Bauling from *The Bed Book of Short Stories* (2010)

"In the Spirit of McPhineas Lata" by Lauri Kubuitsile from *The Bed Book of Short Stories* (2010)

"Fool's Gold" by Tinashe Chidyausiku from *The Bed Book of Short Stories* (2010)

"The Outsider" by Isabella Morris from *The Bed Book of Short Stories* (2010)

"Heaven (or Something Like It)" by Sarah Lotz from *The Bed Book for Short Stories* (2010)

"Spying" by Colleen Higgs from *Looking for Trouble and other Yeoville stories* (2012)

"Vicious Cycle" by Reneilwe Malatji from *Love Interrupted* (2013)

"Prayers" by Makhosazana Xaba from *Running & other stories* (2014)

"The Chameleon House" by Melissa de Villiers from *The Chameleon House* (2015)

"Southbound" by Sandra Hill from *Unsettled and other Stories* (2015)

"Letter to Management" by Julia Martin from *Stray: An Anthology of Animal Short Stories and Poems* (2015)

"The Dream of Cats is all about Mice" by Alex Smith from *Stray: An Anthology of Animal Short Stories and Poems* (2015)

"The Fisherman" by Jolyn Phillips from *Tjieng Tjang Tjerries & other stories* (2016)

"The Good Housekeeping Magazine Quiz" by Jo-Ann Bekker from *Asleep Awake Asleep* (2019)